SELECTED POEMS

BOOKS BY HUBERT MOORE

Hubert Moore's first collection, *Down by a Bicycle*, was published by Hippotamus Press in 1979, when the poet was 45 years old. Since then there have been twelve further full collections: three from Enitharmon Press – *Namesakes* (1988), *Rolling Stock* (1991) and *Left-Handers* (1995); and nine from Shoestring Press – *Touching down in Utopia* (2002), *The Hearing Room* (2006), *Whistling Back (2012), The Bright Gaze of the Disoriented* (2014), *The Tree Line* (2017), *the Feeding-Station* (2019), *Owl Songs* (2019), *Country of Arrival* (2022) and *Hello dear* (2023). His pamphlet *Beautifully Kept Things* (Smith/Doorstep Books, 2003), sixteen poems in memory of his first wife, Diana, was a winner in The Poetry Business Book & Pamphlet Competition.

SELECTED POEMS

HUBERT MOORE

Selected and edited by Lawrence Sail

All rights reserved. No part of this work covered by the copyright herein may be reproduced or used in any means – graphic, electronic, or mechanical, including copying, recording, taping, or information storage and retrieval systems – without written permission of the publisher.

Printed by imprintdigital
Upton Pyne, Exeter
www.digital.imprint.co.uk

Typesetting and cover design by The Book Typesetters
hello@thebooktypesetters.com
07422 598 168
www.thebooktypesetters.com

Published by Shoestring Press
19 Devonshire Avenue, Beeston, Nottingham, NG9 1BS
(0115) 925 1827
www.shoestringpress.co.uk

First published 2023
© Copyright: Hubert Moore
© Photograph of author by Darrie Payne
© Foreword: Lawrence Sail

The moral right of the author has been asserted.

ISBN 978-1-915553-32-4

ACKNOWLEDGEMENTS

Acknowledgements are due to the editors of the following publications, in which a number of the poems have appeared: *Ambit, Argo, Connections, Dream Catcher, Encounter, Equinox, Iron, Lancaster Literature Festival Poems, Lines, Literary Review, London Magazine, London Review of Books, Magma, Modern Poetry in Translation, New Internationalist, New Statesman, Other Poetry, Oxford Magazine, Pink Peace Poetry London, Poetry and Settled Status for All, Poetry Nottingham International, Poetry Wales, Poetry Review, Poetry South East, Prospice, Scintilla, Smith's Knoll, South East Arts Review, South West Review, The Blue Nose Poetry Anthology, The Independent, The Interpreter's House, The Listener, The New Writer, The North, The Printer's Devil, The Rialto, The Salzburg Review, Times Literary Supplement, Tribune, Ver Poets Prize-winners Anthology, Workshop New Poetry.*

'The Ultimate Rendition' was included in the Amnesty anthology *Fire in the Soul*, 'The Believing of Trees' in *Refugee Tales* (Comma), 'Change at Leeds and 'For Five Refugees, One of Them a Piece of Paper' in *A Country of Refuge* (Unbound). 'Murmuration for Eddie' and 'To the Man who Picked my Pocket on the 149' appeared in *Canterbury Festival Poem of the Year (2013)*.

Some of the poems have also been broadcast on the B.B.C. programmes *New Poetry* and *Poetry Now*.

CONTENTS

Foreword   1

from DOWN BY A BICYCLE (1979)

At Night	11
At Long Melford	12
After Her Death	13
Pet	14
'I Have A Pain in Your Head' – Discuss	16
Stance	17
Down by a Bicycle	18
Decorating Incident	19

from NAMESAKES (1988)

In the Field	23
Kentish Maid	24
from Six Graveyard Poems	25
1 Namesakes	25
2 The Receivers	26
3 Edmund-John	27
Before the War	28
Kittens	29
April 16: Day 15, Falklands Crisis	30
Bed-Time Story	31
Kingfishers	32

from ROLLING STOCK (1991)

Crossing the Church	35
Daughter	36
The Night Attendant	37
Shade	38
Rolling Stock	39
For a Wedding Anniversary	40
By the Rhône-Rhine Canal	41
Thursday	42
Villanelle for Elinor	43
In the Back	44
Near Tunbridge Wells	45
Our Master's Voice	46
To a Poetry Editor	48
Rhubarb	50

from LEFT-HANDERS (1995)

4.28	53
At an Exhumation	54
The Man	54
The Woman	54
The Girl	55
Left-Handers	56
Alders	58
Bella	59
Your Poem from India	61
Man Stole Bike	62
Going from Rotherham	63
On Site	64
Virtue	65
from Thirty Sonnets to Diana	66

from TOUCHING DOWN IN UTOPIA (2002)

The Opening	73
The Outside World	74
Cows	76
Open Hut	77
Touching Down in Utopia	78
To a Young Ethiopian TB Patient	84
At the Bottle Bank	85
The Innocents	86
The Screech	88
Full Cry	89
Nightingale	91
Tracking	92
1 In the National Park	92
2 Kingfishers	92
3 On the Road	93
4 Nanda Devi	93
5 The House	94
6 The Creaking Swing	95
Head-On	96
Gentlemen	97
To the Guide at Agorregi Iron-Mill, Northern Spain	98
Cat Sentiment	99
Murmur	100

from BEAUTIFULLY KEPT THINGS (2003)

4 'For want of a nail ...'	105
6 'I have put your trekking sticks ...'	106
8 'There wasn't a warning ...'	107
9 'To rise to every horror ...'	108
10 'The quick-winged kingfisher ...'	109
11 'You saved your notes ...'	110

12	'You left your sandals behind …'	111
14	'It's good things happen …'	112
16	'Beloved …'	113

from THE HEARING ROOM (2006)

Translation	117
How to Listen	118
Music	119
Onion	120
At a Loss	121
For Mack Mehrabian, Baker	123
Approaching Reading	124
At the Cricket	125
I.D.	126
In the Hearing Room	127
At the House of My Father	128
Notice of Arrival	132
On the Border Path	133
Picnic	134
Dream Warfare	135
Locked	136
from the Burning House	137
1 Case	137
5 In the Telling	138
6 The Burning House	138

from WHISTLING BACK (2012)

Back-to-Front	143
Sight-Reading	144
Barefoot	145

Diu	146
Fishmonger	147
Nicety	148
Dimension of the Soul	149
Voice-over	150
Taking the Vow	151
Bat Music	152
No Hands	153
Quail	154
I Believe	155
Ring	156

from THE BRIGHT GAZE OF THE DISORIENTED (2014)

Boy's Name	159
Afghan in London	160
Missed Call	161
Murmuration for Eddie	162
To the Man Who Picked My Pocket on the 149	164
To an Interpreter from A Country at War	165
The Ultimate Rendition	166
Kramm's Iambics	167
Signing up	168
Footsteps	169
In Praise of Rowing	170
Hosing Down	171
Heron Ending	172

from THE TREE LINE (2017)

The Tree Line	175
Arrivals	176
On the Road to Le Blanc	177
Your Voice When You Sing	178
At the Camp Gates	179
For the Detainee Welfare Group Walkers	180
The Believing of Trees	181
Diminuendo	182
Fallen Tree	183
Change at Leeds	184
For Five Refugees, One of Them A Piece of Paper	185
Resistance	186
Setting the Table	187
The Tulip Tree	188

from THE FEEDING-STATION (2019)

At the Feeding-Station	191
The Understanding	192
Route Barrée	193
Burning Diaries	194
At Les Andelys	195
Alongside	196
Walking Along	197
The Sleeping Child	198
What the Story Said	199
Bathroom Taps	200
In the Simple Hall	201
Unseens	202
Wash	203

from OWL SONGS (2021)

Owl	207
Hands	208
In the Alpujarras	209
On a Level-Crossing	210
Waves Breaking	211
Nibbling	212
Being Heard	213
Rain	214
Mud	215
Reflex	216

from COUNTRY OF ARRIVAL (2022)

To Swim	219
Crossing Blind	220
Consultation Document	221
Snakes and Ladders	222
In the Mist	223
All the Difference	224
The Toppling	225
Leave to Remain	226
Gifts from Australia	227
Scars of Not	228
The Heart and the Hearing	229
Unmuted	230
Law	231
Cold Baths	232
The Only Place	233
Field of Vision	234
As Goldfinches	235
Work in Progress	236

from HELLO DEAR (2023)

Hello Dear	239
Long Slow Fall	240
Double-Ended Saw	241
Dawdling	242
Why Would the Road?	243
Balancing Act	244
Weather and News	245
Lime-Grief	246
Butcher's Name	247
Collisions	248
Humanity	249
No Talking Before Breakfast	250
Moon Poem	251
No Fear	252

FOREWORD

"A shilling life will give you all the facts", Auden noted in 'Who's Who' – though it will tell you very little of consequence, as that poem goes on to prove. But it's a Yeats poem, 'The Choice', that Hubert Moore's poetry also calls to mind, with its contention that "The intellect of man is forced to choose / Perfection of the life, or of the work." That is an old enough human conundrum, and the highlighting of the intellect can only be part of the story, since fulfilment is likely to involve the heart as well as the head. And whether it's a matter of intellectual brilliance or moral sensibility, it's at least debatable whether undiluted perfection is ever available. In Moore's case, even a brief account of his life and his poems shows how richly the life and the work inform one another, bearing witness to the remarkable development of a poet who, born in February 1934, was already 45 years old when his first collection was published. No fewer than twelve full collections were to follow.

*

Hubert and his siblings, Alick and Mary, were the children of Will and Joy Moore. Will Moore was Reader in French Literature and Dean of St John's College, Oxford: Joy, radical in her outlook, was a firm Labour supporter. You sense the underpinning of parental influences – the father's capacity for following the sometimes tangential paths of philosophical and academic enquiry; the mother's directness, her firm sense of right and wrong. They will surely have passed on something, too, of an independent outlook predicated on their Congregationalism, with its assertion of each local congregation's right to decide on its own priorities, and the conviction that 'every believer is a priest and … every seeking child of God is given directly wisdom, guidance, power' (Charles Edward Jefferson).

Hubert went to the Dragon School in Oxford, then to Kingswood, Bath – a school providing largely for the sons of Methodists rather than Congregationalists. From there, he won an exhibition to Brasenose College, Oxford, where he read Classical Moderations and Modern Greats. He got a rugby Blue, and also played for South Eastern Counties vs. Australia, as well as captaining his college cricket team.

Following graduation, Hubert embarked on teaching, first at Rose Lane Secondary School, Biggleswade and then, following a year in South Africa, ten more at Sherborne School. In 1960 he married Diana Kelly, and they had four children – Alison, Hilary, Andrew and Elinor. Diana, as radical and principled a thinker as her mother-in-law, worked first as an orthopaedic nurse, and then as a much respected Nurse Educator. She died of cancer in 2001.

By the time his first collection, *Down by a Bicycle*, was published, Hubert and his family had moved to Kent, where he was Head of the English Department at Cranbrook School for thirty-one years, from 1969 to1999 (he and Diana also had a spell as house parents of the school's boarding house). Over the years, voluntary work came to play an increasingly important part in Hubert's life: he was a Listener for the Samaritans (2001–2019); a Visitor to Dover Detention Centre (2002–2011); and a Writing Mentor for the organisation now called Freedom from Torture (2002–2011). In 2009 he moved from Cranbook to Chilham, just north of Canterbury, and in the following year he and Jane Champion, a founder of Kent Refugee Action Network, were married. A simple statement, but a crucial turning-point in both their lives. Hubert had by now stopped teaching: his life was to take an entirely new direction. Jane's friends became his friends. They were many, among them artists, musicians, refugees and refugee supporters from all over the world. As well as direct involvement with new outlooks and causes, there was also extensive travel, often by bicycle. Hubert and Jane cycled all over Europe, and one of their most memorable journeys was a week-long ride alongside the Elbe in East Germany.

Above all, Jane brought to the marriage a quality of love which, in Hubert's own words, "allowed me to find the self I needed to be – to write the poems I needed to write."

*

Critics have praised the truthfulness and the moral dimension present in Moore's work, as well as its precision. Alan Brownjohn was alert early on to its virtues. Reviewing *Namesakes*, Moore's second collection, he praised the poems for "the exactness of their detail" and their "emotional authenticity and frankness". Graham Mort, writing in *North*, admired work that was "carefully crafted", and the poet's "strong sense of integrity". Michael Thomas, describing the poems in *The Hearing Room*, wrote that "Moore is by turns appalled by the excesses of humanity, touched by its capacity for unexpected affection and diverted by its idiosyncrasies". Considering *The Bright Gaze of the Disoriented*, D.A. Prince wrote of "the humanity that is central to his poetry", seeing him as "drawing the whole world into his poems". For Benjamin Hannavy Cousen, writing about *The Feeding-Station*, "Moore's poetry is a sea that proceeds in waves of themes and waves of intensity. Some of the poems are very funny, like a sudden flick of spray; others are deeply moving, not nostalgic but on the brink of the chasm of memory."

*

Many of the key images and themes in Moore's work are the natural outcomes of his middle-class Oxford upbringing, and the pre-war generation to which he belongs. Prominent amongst them are bicycles (not quite ubiquitous, but not far off, common both to his childhood and to his and Jane's travels) and trains, birds, trees, Latin, cricket, water and light, France, his family and ancestors: all these feature as recurrent lifelong waymarks. Something of the momentum of that journeying is caught in the titles of Moore's collections, from *Down by a Bicycle* via, for instance, *Rolling Stock* and *Touching Down in Utopia*, through to the direct speech of *Hello dear*. And the direction of travel is a move away from what might be traditionally regarded as poetic, to something more direct and urgent. Formally, the work develops from a deft neatness, and an exploration of forms such as the villanelle and the sonnet, via poems exploring syllabics and doing without punctuation, to others in stress verse and short lines. Crucially, notwithstanding the occasional use of an out-of-the-way word or phrase, Moore never loses touch with the rhythms and idioms of the spoken language, as his most recent collection again reminds us. Its title, *Hello dear*, could only be direct speech, striking in its very ordinariness – though it's a nice irony that these turn out to be words written, not spoken, the start of a young refugee's message in a bottle.

When it comes to perception of the world at hand, the poems show a marked predilection for the sense of hearing and listening – to birdsong, to background noise, to the assumptions and underlying ambiguities of ordinary speech, transmitted as sound waves that speak to the inquiring mind and the feeling heart, language attuned to nature and to utterance, the quirky slants of dialogue. A typical Moore poem takes a single thought or glimpse of a scene or a phrase heard or overheard, dislocates it, has us consider it from a new angle, subtly re-interprets it. This can be playful, a delighting in the ambivalences of language, alertness deployed in a spirit of modest enquiry that can operate in the interests of wit and humour as effectively as in making a political point.

In what might be termed his middle period, Moore writes wonderfully tender love poems. Their strength is predicated on an exactness which keeps them clear of any sentimentality. And in the later work his use of language, with its potential to be disruptive, indeed essentially non-conformist, reminds us again of its mutable nature. An essential component of freedom, it can also be distorted to serve the diktats of authority, or to confound the demands of natural justice. When it comes to those who have endured imprisonment and torture, finding a voice – a language – able to articulate the trauma of their experience is a difficult but essential element in their recovery – a process that can be greatly helped by companionship and mentoring, as much as by practical support and poems. Much of Moore's later work focuses, with growing intensity and indignation, on the plight of refugees, prisoners and detainees.

*

Against the bleak intemperance of zealots Moore sets acceptance of what Louis MacNeice, saw (in his poem 'Snow') as a world "crazier and more of it than we think, /Incorrigibly plural". But what is the response to the charge, made by some, that activism is as monolithic and uncompromising as the authoritarianism it opposes? This viewpoint posits a false moral equivalence, of course – but in terms of his poems part of Moore's answer is to adopt a strategy of open possibilities, a stance exemplified by what he calls 'mildness', a word that he uses a number of times in one form or another. In his thinking, such qualifications as 'maybe', 'might', 'might have', 'seem', 'all I know is…' are evidence not of being tentative or uncertain, but an acknowledgement of the need to keep areas of speculation and enquiry available to the reader. An inclusivity that allows for differing facets of the same question (and for humour) is an essential component of freedom and tolerance. In this sense it is the very slipperiness of language, its ability to outflank attempts at prescription, that works to keep the world open. But how does religious belief, a subject broached a number of times in the poems, fare in this perspective? Moore keeps the matter on the horizon, but settles for a bearing somewhere between agnosticism and apparent disbelief, though it could be argued that his respect and affection for so many aspects of the world and its inhabitants, his feeling for those in need, his celebration of human love amount to a sense of hope that borders on faith.

*

Considering the overall development of his work, a collection that stands out as key is his fifth book, *Touching Down in Utopia*. It shows a great increase in range and confidence, with a new emphasis on the world of work and the everyday, alongside poems set in Ethiopia, Sudan and India, where his wife, Diana, spent her childhood. That book's successor, *Beautifully Kept Things*, stands out in an altogether different way. Its intensely moving love poems remembering Diana, which combine the philosophical and the personal, show an awareness of mortality that finds its counterpart much later, in *Hello dear*, with its poems in memory of friends and contemporaries and its conjuring of the flickering alternations of the dead, their presence and their absence.

From the next book on, *The Hearing Room*, it is the powerful poems about victims of torture and the sufferings of asylum seekers that dominate, themes pursued with equal directness in *The Bright Gaze of the Disoriented*, *The Tree Line* and *The Feeding Station*. After that, in its way *Owl Songs* seems something of a hinge or hiatus, as much as *Beautifully Kept Things*, its 53 poems (each of thirteen lines) delightful miniatures reminding the reader of Moore's gifts for observation as well as gentle speculation. Then, *Country of Arrival* tellingly considers the impact and challenge of refugees for those on whose shores they land. As 'In the Mist' concludes,

> Dear
> refugees in the mist, walk
>
> on water across to us,
> save us, save us from us.

Hello dear, Moore's most recent book, is dedicated "to people who reject hostility, welcomers everywhere". Along with *Country of Arrival*, it makes for, not exactly a coda, but an affirmation of the poet's closest beliefs as well as his writing practice. As Moore writes:

> Over my last few collections I've become an increasingly frequent user of the wonderful word, 'you'. 'You' ... may be my wife, my brother, my son, one of my daughters, a friend. It may be me, talking to myself. I find poems can only come into existence if they are imagined as being said to someone. In my case the people addressed are ultimately the readers, you.

In selecting from more than 620 poems written over a period of nearly half a century, I have sought to represent both the scope of Moore's work and the nature of its development. Inevitably, personal preference has played its part, but so has the need to achieve an accurate balance. It has been particularly challenging to choose between so many compelling poems about refugees and victims of torture – poems that certainly express the poet's concern, yes, but of course no amount of concern could in itself guarantee the poems' success: here and elsewhere the reader has the pleasure of enjoying a poet really talented as a writer, and one remarkably free of self-regard.

*

I am very grateful to John Lucas for his unfailing encouragement; and to the typesetters and book designers, Nat and Rachael Ravenlock. Most of all, I want to thank Hubert Moore who, not well enough to undertake the work himself, entrusted to me the making of this book. That has been a delight and an honour.

Lawrence Sail, August 2023

from DOWN BY A BICYCLE (1979)

AT NIGHT

Breath
– in the burr of next-room sleepers –
catches, suddenly high

catches at something:
from the dead of a far wood
cackles,

then lilts off
to a new tree
and proceeds to riddle it.

All night
cheek and temple
hollow and hollow and hollow.

AT LONG MELFORD

Rabbits, in the glow
of a round church-window. Three of them,
putting their heads together.

Is it trouble? They look like
a group of friends-Romans-and-countrymen
lending an ear to each other.

Of ears they've enough to go round:
three ears between the three of them, and not
one rabbit goes short either.

Every ear-tip tickles
the same head it hears for; every ear-end
is both ear-root and ear-feather.

Ear-locked they're one,
the three of them. Our guide-book says
it's the Trinity. I'm not sure whether

I believe in the Trinity.
Father I see, and son – and then
any holy having-the-ear-of-them mother.

AFTER HER DEATH

I

She is of course absent: not
sitting here in her chair,
toes turned inwards, back bent
over the writing-table she makes of her knees.

Absent, so that she's not
sitting here in the chair,
in the curious cramped position – pigeon-toed –
I find myself sitting in.

II

I might be praying:
head held between hands,
the bed become lectern and elbow-rest,
the bedroom floor knee-mortifying.

Until the newspaper
is picked through and I haul
legs gone dead, strange white foot-flesh
in for the night. This is her

last illness cats-eyeing
back through the dark at me,
her blood opening and closing its claws.
I might be praying.

PET

Yes. From Africa, eleven days ago.
Sex: female. Diet: salads suit her.
Care: once a week a little water
washes ants from her shell. So

now we know – or would do if
only they could say how old
our lettuce-loving, lately much-travelled
she-tortoise is. That tentative-

looking totter, for example,
across my grass-patch, are those her
first eleven-day-wonder
steps ever? Or is the poor soul

nosing each stalk, following
some faint trail here and there
and then no further? We've no idea
whether she's coming or going.

Coming/going, anyway,
she makes quite good progress
/hardly at all advances
up/down our morning tea-tray

/untracked outback of
a garden. She even has the grace
/tortoise-tigerishness
to nibble a little/heave

headfuls from the half
tomato that we offer her.
But if, assured, we go too near
/far for her, she swallows herself

at a gulp; and we, pet her
with poems, stroke the tortoise-
shell that she securely lounges
/lies cowering the other

side of though we may – we're
nothing to her. Yet can harden
too: proud possessors of an African
tortoise, marvellous/mere.

'I HAVE A PAIN IN YOUR HEAD' – DISCUSS

We had a week to do it: make,
over pub lunches, our first mockery –
'Is this by any chance your finger
in my pie?', 'The Philosophy tutor
is a pain in the neck. Discuss' – ;
in midweek listen to a lecture;
on the sixth day corner a friend – 'This
essay title, what's the point of it?' –
at 10 p.m. on the seventh, write.

After that we had twenty years
in which to go off blindly in pairs,
and not to write a line, not even
discuss it; then, and only then, one
of us might look and cry out seeing
beyond his folded hands (this vein
of hers in his wrist) the pain of being
twenty and himself, lifted
bodily, there in the other's head.

STANCE

I know that stance of yours, half-confronting,
shy. You are going to tell me latest cricket scores
laboriously noted; or have you cooked one of my
favourite dishes? At trivial frontier-points of ours
you stand so, your left foot advancing
a welcome half-step into my territory.

Wife, I recognize you. Entitled 'Kore,
Sixth Century B.C.' years ago you were.
Our school text book asked us to notice
the almost amused challenge the sculptor
had given the eyes, the way he had made the drapery
fall back from where the left leg would be; this

stepping out attitude was a new, nearer-to-human
persuasion of stone by the artist. Months he
must have worked at it with the chipping persistence
of a person's ordinary care for another person. Maybe
we have from him too something of blinding appreciation
of a quite unsuspected new point of balance.

DOWN BY A BICYCLE

He walked calmly along.
There was no reason why he shouldn't
– that way, that hour of the day –
walk so. While he was walking

he looked about him. Then he
stooped: down by a bicycle
against the public wall
left propped as casually

as ever he walked up
the road past it. Now his
fingers were steadying themselves
on the front tyre valve-cap:

he twisted and felt it go
loose to him. Pfit. The last
air seeped out and left
the fat tyre hollow.

Nothing to it. Nothing
but how the wheel's rib-cage
took the new dead-weight on it
and he walked calmly along.

DECORATING INCIDENT

I cut myself on a swallow's nest.
Its best part must have chipped
away from the wall against
which my ladder stood propped.
This bit was left, sharp as rust.

Into the mid-air of my property
it had been built, and I had cut
my finger on it. Blood suddenly
hopped from the hole and fell flat
on the concrete path under me.

That's how the rest of me'd go, hadn't
my ladder the house to lean
up against. I'm wise, obedient –
except that again and again
I flit back with an incident:

building out, hoping my mud will stick,
thinking any odd thing magic.

from NAMESAKES (1988)

IN THE FIELD

We ran from Ancient History
to the cricket ground, getting there
soon after the war ended.

Out of the sacked city onto the plain
the beardless barbarians
as quickly as possible came

and, being prevented,
tunnelled under the encirclement –
the tall men standing, the benches –

and there, past sandwich boxes,
bottles, people's lower legs,
there, in front of our noses,

was the whole of the then-known
world, its neat green provinces
mown out, its figures

golden – Hammond, someone mentioned;
I noticed Agricola,
quite near us, sauntering

round his boundary, still
like the rest of them making
history as though it were hay,

hardly glancing outwards, over
their shoulders – though encircled
by us who lay in wait for them.

KENTISH MAID

She's always there, the thin, trembly lady
I've been visiting two years now.
Every Wednesday I come in
and she's halfway through George and Weedon
Grossmith's *The Diary of a Nobody*.

I sit, her hands shake, and we renew
last week's conversation: how intelligent
I must be, coming from Oxford; how
I can spare the time for a visit
with all the books I have to get through.

I was too much for her one Wednesday.
I sat, her hands shook, her arms
stubbed at her pages. She couldn't find
the tongue inside her head. I couldn't…
She was too much for me that Wednesday.

Next week when I came, she was better.
Her book lay loose in her lap. Early
chapters that for years she'd shivered through
warmed to her touch: the family move
to Plymouth, from somewhere still quite near –

Yalding, in Kent. I said the only
other person I'd ever heard of
living in Yalding was a writer
called Edmund Blunden. She said Edmund
was the eldest of the family.

from SIX GRAVEYARD POEMS

1   Namesakes

My namesakes, the children
of JAMES MOORE – Alfred, Marianne,
Esther, George, Levy, Mark,
Walter, Ann, and Ellen –

who together, in 1860, erected
(though George was the moving spirit)
this weighty, versified stone,
seem to have made

more fuss of the dying
of their prolific father
than their next-grave neighbours
the Relfs made of burying

ROBERT RELF, who departed this life
on December 15th 1884,
or, four years after him,
MARY ANN RELF, his wife.

Despite these verses, it's Relf
not Moore I write for: his
unfussy death, and that rare gift
of rhyming with oneself.

2   The Receivers

Thieves came: broke glass and went
uproariously off with this
Gent's Extra Large Bicycle
by Percy W. Evernden,
cycle-maker and -mender
for 60 years, Paddock Wood, Kent.

They couldn't sell this. One teetered
a figure of almost 8. Thrown,
they kicked in the wheel-spokes,
buckled the wheels with a car-jack,
then tipped the bicycle
over the wall of the graveyard

where the headstones
of CHARLES IDEN EVERNDEN, saddler,
and DAMARIS, his wife,
Percy's long-dead grandparents,
were sitting bolt upright in bed
half expecting just such nonsense.

3   Edmund-John

On his gravestone it says
he climbed to the top of Mont Blanc:
EDMUND-JOHN CLARK was one of the few
enterprising travellers to achieve this.

In the late 1830s and the 1840s
there must have been plenty
who came faithfully past this gravestone
every Sunday and didn't think twice

about that infinitely higher
climb Edmund-John was attempting
now he was dead. The 1836 engraver
couldn't of course tell whether

we'd think climbing Mont Blanc a preamble
or a mere feat; he simply engraved.
We can believe if we can: Edmund-John
has enterprise and will travel.

BEFORE THE WAR

I think my mother said
Hugh Gaitskell, John Betjeman, C.H. Gadney and she
were in the same class together at school,
as eight-year-olds in Oxford
before the First World War started.

I can certainly remember
my mother's distress when Gaitskell died.
She said Gaitskell represented her.
Her laughter too – I can reach out and touch
her middle-class Oxford laughter

there on the shelf: *Collected Poems*
of John Betjeman. And C.H. Gadney, the famous
rugby referee who died last year?
Once I managed to meet him, asked
"Do you remember Joy Holmes?"

"Oh yes, Joy." I think he really
did remember. Was it true then
that C.H. Gadney was a little in love
with my mother, as I think she thought
and as I now need it to be?

KITTENS

Two left: we called religiously
at every door in the village, asking.
Still two left: one nondescript, blackish;
its brother black all over but for
a prim white bib. My father
christened this one "John Wesley".

The water-butt, barrel-chested, tall
as a grown man: we boys clung to it,
watched the thick black rain roughen
and gleam when my father drowned them.
Five years later he sent us both
to a Methodist boarding school.

We're nothing special now: if anything,
Anglican. At least it's dignified –
till a hymn's announced and an old tune
floods back: a hand presses gently down
on the head and lo! through clouds comes Charles
Wesley, brother of John, descending.

APRIL 16: DAY 15, FALKLANDS CRISIS

Amazingly, all over again, my mother's
worst fears, most hated language: on TV,
in newspapers, amongst friends even, fighting
talk of old, peace-loving animals now
unsheathing their claws, and of the beauty
of warships and certain winged predators.

No one, she would have said, could be so warlike
without wanting war. I've been asking round. Almost
all my fellow 1930s and 40s seedlings,
gnarled now, square their shoulders, Yes, would
fight for the Falklands. I've been thinking
maybe my mother was just an eccentric.

Till today, her birthday again, another
day nearer us answering force
with force, when *The Guardian's* Country Diary
has a piece about Bedgebury Forest, in Kent,
where apparently there's a notice saying:
'All trees on the left come from the same mother.'

BED-TIME STORY

Would I please
put more experience into my voice?
When the people
said sad things to each other,
why didn't I put
some experience into it,
like her mother?

KINGFISHERS

Waiting by the pond for the kingfisher,
waiting for her to come breezing up
through deep ponds
of sunlight, through flickering willows,
in our kingfisher-blue Fiesta,

I sit still as pond-water, not still –
a cloud catches its breath, willows
go weak at the knees
at the flicker between them of
kingfisher, kingfisher, kingfisher.

Now I'll announce it to everyone:
how this wife came up and sat
inches from me
(by the pond, by the road through the trees).
I could have held out my hand.

from ROLLING STOCK (1991)

CROSSING THE CHURCH

Some seem born to it. They could cross
the gleaming track from the nave to the altar
blindfold.

Look, no hands even. Now they're squaring
their shoulders eastwards, gravely inclining
their heads;

and now they're over, strolling off amidst pews,
leaving one at least of us standing
helpless

as ever to help the children we were,
who anyway couldn't be helped,
born

trespassers, laying our ears
to the cold steel of the track, hearing
the rail

singing the song that we hoped for,
five miles off, centuries still
for us,

knees bare on the flinty stone,
heads where the wheels would be rolling –
then scrambling safely across.

DAUGHTER

It's dark still as we drive five
simple miles to catch her train.
No one else on the roads: we dazzle
nothing, nothing dazzles us. We let
our headlights nose in the hedges
a hundred yards ahead. The moon,
in open sky to our left, lays
cottages flat in their own
front gardens, burns trees black
on the white water of orchards,
and angles in undipped, unblinking
on my beloved passenger,
awake now, going calmly to work.

Driving home I find I'm thinking
who's this behind me somewhere
to my right not quite following
– there's no light in the mirror –
yet not so road-hogging or rash
as to overtake me?

THE NIGHT ATTENDANT

At home, on winter nights
when no one else is crossing
(Southampton - Le Havre or Cherbourg,
Portsmouth - St Malo), he waits

grimly indulgent, alone
in his cabin, till she's way
offshore, past The Needles,
past the red eyes of the buoys,

then tip-toes in, can hear
through the steady jar of the engines
there are passengers sleeping –
this one under the wing

of her shoulder, hands clasped
to her collar-bone, face
abandoned. He closes her book;
turns the bedside light off; even

gives her the same sleep twice –
sits at his desk from midnight
to 1 a.m., adjusts his watch, sits
at his desk from midnight to 1 a.m.

At dawn he draws back the curtains.
Morning after morning he shows her
her first sight of land. Look,
she can see houses quite clearly.

SHADE

Bedded with sleepers once, long since
leaf-moulded, the grand carriageway
tunnelling up through the trees
from the great house
to where the great gates were,

now an almost subterranean
public footpath, up which
my father walked halfway, slowly,
savouring the eeriness.
A connoisseur of shade,

its furred-up stillnesses, the close
grain of its silence: thick of the air
you could stand up a birch-tree in
or an elderly man,
tall, squaring his shoulders

at the sudden, oil-less wheels
of a woodpecker passing.
Unless that's the cry shades make
when, halfway up,
someone looks back at them.

ROLLING STOCK

Cross the canal, drop bicycles in the hedge,
perch on the railwaymen's stile. Eyes
at fire-box level, eyes on fire,
watch the tank-engines cannoning
coal-trucks, brick-trucks, empty carriages
into their lines; craning forwards, dare them
to do their tricks for us – grind brakes,
wheeze steam suddenly, whistle
with nothing to whistle at, turn sixpences
into shillings as they grate past on our line.

Come home, the three of us, to various
named characters: Grandpa – the billiards Grandpa –
starting from nothing, from a difficult in-
off-white, then a cannon, then an easy
cannon to come; Grandpa Holmes whistling
at meal-times; Crowe, married to Muriel,
twice his size; and Uncle Percy, who,
one Harvest Festival service, chose for himself
from the pile on the window-ledge an apple,
and cracked it open while we froze in prayer.

Hear such loose-linking 1940s incidents
shake couplings, whistle, then drag off
into the distance. Hear the bouncing drop
of a signal, points scuttling over, a tank-
engine like some tinpot deity
blasting off, then, wheels gently insisting,
throbbing along our line, three rigid
carriages glide by. See, from the top rung
of our perch in the marshalling-yard, craning
towards us, ourselves, ourselves, ourselves.

FOR A WEDDING ANNIVERSARY

She goes downstairs and the paper bag
she's left on the bed in the almost
empty room takes thirty years un-
crinkling. Letters printed across it –
the name and address of a woolshop –
creak apart to the latest shape
of her knitting: like the name carved
on the bark of the person she was
before marrying, its letters high
and wide and bodiless now, stretched
on the slow quake of her making.

BY THE RHÔNE-RHINE CANAL

Fingers entwining, maybe
an arm thrown over the shoulders,
these huge-limbed chestnut-trees
make all day every day evening
along our stretch of canal.

Here nothing is moving. Water
brims in its water-trough; traffic
of time as of barges is obsolete.
All evening we sit, the two of us,
huge-limbed, weightless, by the canal,

as though, by opening sluices,
one or the other couldn't easily,
aimlessly drift down the map, through
widening gorges, to the river's mouth-
watering delta, les Bouches du Rhône,

or, merely locking off water,
float clean through Germany, further
and further northwards, high on the tide
of purer and purer Rhinewater,
up the sheer face of the map.

THURSDAY

Thursday is Jueves, the day
when the water is due.
Castor has it on Monday,
Pedro on Tuesday, Félix on Wednesday,
then on Thursday…

they'll give us a whole day
of the mountain's water –
like a weekend for two in Paris
or drinks on the house
or, though it leaves us again
and again at midnight, the gift
of suddenly knowing:

how, at the top of the woods,
at a casual undamming,
a boulder of water will rise
from the stream-bed and fall
over and over, any-
where, down into any
aching throat of your land
you happen to choose, green

will spread like a blush each
side of the ditches you've drawn
between fig-trees, the wrinkled
cheeks of your plums will fatten
like children's, your poplars
will ripple Arroyo, Arroyo
and throw back their leaves, and even
the dust in the veins of this
poem may turn – mañana, mañana,
Jueves mañana – into mud.

VILLANELLE FOR ELINOR

Perhaps a villanelle will do the trick
for me, if not for you in Africa,
crossing the border into Mozambique.

Love, you know it's a war zone? Every week
we hear of raids and casualties out there.
Perhaps a villanelle will do the trick.

Of course you had to go, you had to take
the path across the mountains. Dear daughter,
crossing the border into Mozambique,

your boots too tight for you, your old ruck-sack
on its last knees, you said in your letter,
perhaps a villanelle will do the trick.

What ease we wrapped you in for you to break
from it so vibrantly: courting danger,
crossing the border into Mozambique,

you stretch yourself, and me on such a rack,
O activist, parental pace-maker,
perhaps a villanelle will do the trick.
Crossing the border into Mozambique.

IN THE BACK
('Had he his hurts before?')

Hurts lately grown honourable:
ridiculous, Old Siward's first
terrified thought when, flushed with goodness,
they told him his son was gone –
dead at the hand of the tyrant.
The boy could still be God's soldier
so long as the wounds…The wounds
weren't in the back, were they?

This wound is in the back.
We see the boy running, then,
inside his shirt, this mudball
erupting as the rifle's patience
cracks. Natural as tears the politics
of shootings: youthfulness, innocence,
the back-wound, and the broken English
of the dead Palestinian's father.

They need us there as witnesses.
There where they draw the sheet back,
behind the frail partition, the whole
world noses in and sees dark hair,
the hardly stiffened neck, and a hole
next to the spine. Yes, he'll serve:
look how the shoulders bare their blades
through the thin shirt of the skin.

NEAR TUNBRIDGE WELLS

Watched 'Cry Freedom' again last night:
the Crossroads rioting, Biko's death, Sharpeville etc
depicted
as harshly as ever of course
but different now that Mandela is free.

Re-winding was different too: to see
bullets back in their rifles, a massacre
retracted
as though it could somehow be –
as though yesterday never happened

at a Belfast stadium where, sound
switched to a murmur, the cameras
inspected
the broken flesh of rioting
football fans. It could have been Devon

for colour, red weeping from sandstone;
for tears, it could have been any
impacted
rockface or manface in Britain.
This morning the mind's eye's full of it:

winding, re-winding, the place I inhabit
is Capetown and Belfast, merely the world
contracted.
Here chair-leg and cricket-bat handle
are each a policeman's baton.

OUR MASTER'S VOICE

We must have caught the crackling somewhere
along Belbroughton; or where Banbury
turns into Bardwell if, late as usual,
we went in bare-faced, through the main gates.

Heads down – we might have been blindfold –
we'd be just about bicycling into
whatever had ghosted coldly up
from the Cherwell during the night,

just about passing the blackened ring
where one of our Lancasters fell
one Sunday afternoon on a placid
North Oxford house, when through the mist

the voice came to us, talking us in
from our childhoods, our Summertown
gardens where the heat of the sun
met the heat off the sunlit brickwork.

Star-jumps they were doing, and we
leaned our bikes on the Maths hut and jumped
like stars, then changed with the rest
to slow, hands-on-hips trunk-rolling.

Clockwise from nine a.m. we rolled,
while the corky trunk of the man
in the playground-pulpit rolled anti-
clockwise – us he was in a mirror,

making men of us, slowly coiling
the thin strings of our back-muscles
(he had rope – we'd seen it – coiled
in the bursting bags on his calves).

Some last days – of a term, of a whole
boyhood – he'd be his crackling self,
except that we for once were to keep
our wits about us and obey him

only when he was O'Grady. 'Arms
raise', he'd snap. Arms twitching to obey,
we'd stand there waiting for 'O'Grady
says "Arms raise"'. Then we'd raise arms,

jump like stars in opposition, leave school,
march, vote against Suez, the Falklands War,
the Bomb, bombing Gaddafi, Star Wars,
Public Schools, Prep Schools, and Belbroughton Road.

TO A POETRY EDITOR

Every Sunday in term-time at four p.m.
young men would come, like lambs –
little marching lambs on their college ties
with flags over their shoulders –
to the slaughter: suited, blazered,
up from Marlborough, Merchant Taylor's,
Haileybury – though, even in the 1940s,
the drawing-room held its breath
when one young man, under fire
from my mother, admitted to Eton.

The Dean and family at home:
three children somewhere there, not knowing
what they were thinking; their father,
his Yorkshire vowels still, like his eyebrows,
bristling after fifteen years down South;
his wife, clear-eyed anti-élitist,
daughter of Oxford, Oxford mother
extraordinary, moving graciously
amongst young men, pouring them tea
like mild unanswerable questions.

In summer no one was safe,
not even when tea was over. Quoits
in the garden: a rubber ring and a net,
a parapet rather, chest high, the height
of my eyes. My brother crushed the ring
in his hands and watched it wobbling
back into shape as it fell; I
flung at the young men's throats, dared them,
down the gleaming guns of my eyes,
to take this next untakable one.

Scholars, schoolboy heroes, Blues, a Welsh
International once – I can feel
the shine in my eyes as we shook hands
after I'd lost. One's a judge now,
there are public school headmasters,
editors, dons – still holding court,
the other side of the net, at Eton,
at Oxford. I'd fling the ring now,
only I wonder, Is there any chance
of you taking this untakable one?

RHUBARB

Like young beans in July – runners rather than dwarfs –
this early rhubarb snaps into bits in your fingers,
all shin-bone and thigh-bone its pale hockey-stick legs.

Yet not so much legs as curious pink antennae
that somebody's done so well, through the winter months,
to stretch – the sky's the limit – through peat or straw

in a bottomless upturned bucket, that now, poor loves,
they're going for 65p a pound, the scholarship set,
fast-forwarded to Blundell's, Ampleforth, Eton.

from LEFT-HANDERS (1995)

4.28

At the point
of what seems to have been
a knife on a lavatory wall:
WOMEN ARE SHIT BUT I LOVE DAWN.

Last night I set
the alarm. 4.28 she's due.
Already I'm wondering
what sort of gown she'll be wearing.

At 4.27 a choir
of one is singing in a bush.
No light, let alone radiance;
there's not a rosy finger to be seen.

Something though.
Something the leaves' ears are pricked for.
Something the black
hollyhock standing quietly beside me

stiffens at.
When the light comes
let's not name it: scratch,
if we must, with a pen or the point

of a knife,
its cool clean time of the night
on a page or a lavatory wall:
I LOVE 4.28 a.m.; DAWN IS SHIT.

AT AN EXHUMATION

The Man

There's weather round the corner
so no disrespect he keeps
his hands inside an armless
body-warmer otherwise
he has erected spine and
soiled old head on duty on
his bristling tenterhooks he
hates it and he wants to see
the bodies so he presses
back his knees his neat twin feet
are saying simple prayers
he's cordoned off but he can
stand however long and at
his own attention frankly

The Woman

She is about to dance at
any moment there could be
a wheelbarrow and drumming
and she's ready for her poise
I think or else the way she
squares to it sincerely that's
what's so beautiful she has
her head upraised her arms are
windproof but they're opening
her big legs lighten there's an
envelope she ought to post
can wait she hasn't ever

seen unearthed not live someone's
poor love grievous bodily

The Girl

She's come to this to
edging forward for
a sight a whiff her
arms are folded but
her legs would go so
would her eyes her smile
her tilted face give
everything for this
to stumble forwards
O run lumpishly
through ropes policemen
stench society
throw up herself and
be the murdered girls

LEFT-HANDERS

What oddity were we looking for?
(my mother, on realising
all her children had opted

for left-handed spouses). Left
elbows held like an injury,
left wrists cocked, they'd sit –

a son- and two daughters-in-law –
aslant at her table, writing,
pushing their pens south-east
across tilted south-west-facing
paper. Not that she minded
or would have felt other than joy

at this second daughter-in-law
at seven in the morning right-hand-
driving me off to the station

for work, stopping outside it,
emerging high-heeled, smart-suited –
the engine ticking over –

while I get out, go left
to right round the back of the car,
kiss her and drive off home.

There's no urgency now. Against
the thrust of commuting car
after car, I let the road take me,

thinking of how, amongst
all those right-armers, my father
bowled slow left arm round the wicket.

ALDERS

One of the alders stands exactly like you,
or rather two of them do.

No one could say that you loll or prop
your weight on a hip,

yet when you draw yourself up to take
that long critical look

at something I've done – cut a tree down,
re-hung a picture – one

of your legs (your left, my right) falters
loose at the knee, while the other's

the perfect alder, tapering, straight.
Love, startlingly upright

you who mean what you say
and say I should re-hang inches away

from where I've already re-hung,
and believe in something

balanced and final and good, inching
upwards towards it, branching

and branching – love, one of the alders
(your left, my right) falters.

BELLA

Upper V we were, all male, expecting
some sort of victory. Next year –
if none of our forces yielded –
we'd be Upper IIIA; then Upper I,
pride of the then-known world.

We advanced across open territory.
Every day we captured a village
or enemy fort. Across the walls
of our high-windowed classroom
coloured flags charted our progress.

For nouns of the First Declension,
a feminine colour, pale green –
though a few males like Nauta
also had feminine endings.
We didn't care, we declined them.

Verbs were scarlet, purple, maroon,
according to Conjugation. First
we marched through Amo, forcing
its principal parts to surrender;
next week we'd conjugate Rego.

One lunch-hour, though, our master
being absent, three of our army
climbed the wall to the window-ledge
and stood exposed on the rampart,
trembling, pale, with no clothes on.

Not for many years, however,
were traitors discovered amongst us.
For, our master approaching,
we returned as quickly as possible
to that beautiful girl, wars.

YOUR POEM FROM INDIA

India slows and stops a few shouts nothing more.
No sweat so far (for us back here no sweat).
Peak heat you say in somewhere poor

when quick a Keralan girl your
neighbour going south twists from her seat –
India slows and stops a few shouts nothing more –

claps her hands at the window. Look she shrieks look here
look man on track head body separate.
Peak heat you say in somewhere poor.

You look out too but now an older
man is lifting up the head. He holds it –
India slows and stops a few shouts nothing more –

by the hair and tenderly. In your letter
he doesn't howl, he holds the head upright.
Peak heat you say in somewhere poor,

not here and yet, O tender other
older men and fathers, hear the quiet:
India slows and stops a few shouts nothing more.
Peak heat you say in somewhere poor.

MAN STOLE BIKE

Man stole bike to visit poorly son.
Didn't have money, stole this mountain
bike, rode it nine miles, saw poorly son.
Owner told police, police arrived,
arrested man, ex-miner, 21.
Bike, worth £200, found damaged.
Man denied all knowledge: mountain bike
went perfectly for him free-wheeling
up the hills as well as down. Man got
conditional discharge; had to cough up
compensation though – £60 plus
costs plus quite a bollocking of course.
It didn't pay to steal, man would know
to take the bus in future: bus fare
subsidised, concessions, benefits,
support, etc. What did man expect?
Man, expectations nil, had stolen
against others, law, morality.
Man, 21, rose up on high nine miles
to visit poorly son on mountain.

GOING FROM ROTHERHAM

That was it they had remanded him
he hadn't been convicted he must
go inside the locking escort van
from court to prison from Rotherham
to Wolds on Humberside from drinking
vodka in a water-bottle to
choking on his vomit on remand
inside a locking cubicle which
no one thought to look in and by then
acute intoxication had so
sickened him in head in custody
that he'd inhaled it no one noticed
but the brain damage was done and now
he'd not get back to Rotherham or
pre-Rotherham the inquest jury
said that lack of care contributed
but care the ethic the profession
had been privatised no stopping on
the motorway the man's collapse
his sick his hopelessness they didn't
want to know bad business lack of care
locked in a private cubicle on
M62 the eastbound carriageway
where he had choked on it the damage

ON SITE

Even work Sunday mornings bloody
builders hammering at least this mid-
September misty one they've left their
music beating someone else's brains
the two of them up ladders fixing
roof-beams no one else about their soft
furred outlines high on overtime they've
no idea they ghost the saintliness
of working bloody builders nailing
with little taps then big decisive
hits our sentiments until they pause

for more nails or more uprightness so
now the nut-trees between us and them
can sob their fill and now from one saint
up a column to another there
can boom huge intimacies someone's
wife has gone three children too a man
called Merv says course they'd have them got their
own kids though Merv knew she'd go shook him
and Jenny rigid to be honest they'd
been at each other in the fog they
nail with taps and big decisiveness

at lunch they find the warm brown crackling
underneath them cob-nuts God they're sweet
they're deep in them now the clusters God they're
fucking sweet they make a pile for home
sweet builders sweetly fucking builders

VIRTUE

Saw Mary Magdala last night I
can't have done there was no question this
was Mary who had seven devils
extracted the immoral Mary
rather cramped she came inside the head
of someone she was tickled to be
there at all I think and not a bit
resentful what we do so grossly
men I mean itching our itch of need
our disrespect was nothing to her
it was where she poured her separate
pale serenity all those chapters
she had gone along until towards
the end of every gospel Mary
would be there on her knees with water
saints betrayers martyrs she'd flow through
their toes she'd cup their heels her cool high
tide would wash across their beaches I
like her best of all the characters
she said last night there were no limits
no conditions there was love I said
I couldn't she was in the Bible

from THIRTY SONNETS TO DIANA

1

Like rain waking you up in India
my poem sounded being printed out.
Down in your continent you mumble about
corrugated iron roofs and rains being heavier
there. I wake you again, in prose. You've got
a drenching day ahead of you of Nursing
Theory, its flood of abstracts immersing
you so mildly you scarcely notice it.

I do though. When you come home, I want
to write a sonnet – eight and six – pointed
like an elbow on a table, obstinate,
muscular, clenched; and, love, so insistent
that you hear its words through corrugated
roofs, out there in India, a child at night.

5

Oh you love parameters, not just them
but the word for them and the way your hands
can lock a space off, rigid as book-ends
letting the books stand tall. Drifting, at some
unscripted point between work and work, I'm
deep in the paper and you're in the act
of measuring, palm to palm, the exact
space you have given your students to roam.

And now, of course, you want a definition,
a precise definition of the prefix
'para'. All I vaguely remember

is us once walking together between
reed-hedge and reed-hedge, my sex and your sex,
παρα τον ποταμον, by the river.

7

I can confirm what Hardy says is true:
that when in the evening the long sun lies
on the earth flush with its fiery grasses,
you can see past the trickling veins right through
the ear of a rabbit. Pity Hardy's
anathema to you. I think you hate
not so much fate or misfortune as what
gives these such power: you hate passiveness.

Hence your bedside reading, currently Schon's
The Reflective Practitioner or *How
Professionals Think in Action*. Rather
you than me. You know I think reflection's
everything. Well, now I'm not so sure, now
that I've seen the light through a rabbit's ear.

13

Sunning ourselves, any moment sailing
(wasn't it that late September Sunday
when – panic – they said the sea was 'agitée'?)
we watched, from the next deck up, men coiling
our mooring-ropes. I saw then why you'd said
ten days before we crossed (you'd come home brisk
and practical straight from work to your desk)
'Unanchored', 'unanchored thoughts in your head';

and how, in open sea at your desk, the last
of the light had gone, and coldly staring
mountain ranges had come drifting by,
and you, buoyant, unagitated, crossed
from one white cliff to the other, mooring
to mooring, ropes coiled, anchor high and dry.

22

For years I thought (starling, sleek blue-green
on the bird-table) that the white life-boat
we children sailed in our bath must have got
its name from a starling, a rare grey one.
Then somebody said that the chipped old faithful
that ferried soap from the groin's beaches
to the coral reef of the toes was Grace
Darling, the name of a girl after all.

The boat's long gone. I've missed it. I don't say
Grace, can't handle the abstracts, Love, Honour,
Beauty, etc. Don't even say Darling.
The white rocks of your knees, the faint blue way
up your thigh that a cliff-path takes – yet poor
you Di have to make do with Grey Starling.

28

Sleep on this (prescribing before sleeping),
sleep on the fact that whereas human bone,
especially, you say, the bone of women,
wastes while we're resting (rich juice seeping
while you dream your schemes), the bones of bears
(your light's on now, now you're truly alight)

interestingly (you love saying that) get
denser and denser while they sleep whole winters.

Somewhere there's a poem. I wake to find
a polished three-foot rod of moonlight
entering your head: from a thin sliver
of window left imperfectly curtained
to the white of your collar-bone, the white
of your head, love, under its head of hair.

30

Waking at 2 it seems to me your knees
have made a cool high altar and our duvet
drapes it. Go to sleep, you say. I think you say
you are reading about juniper trees.
I don't ask all next day about the juniper.
OK we're strangers, we don't communicate.
I still don't ask. By evening it's too late.
Were you awake at 2? I'm not sure you were.

And then I see your smoke, your book at least.
'Juniper is potent in dreams', says some
dreamer by the name of Thistleton-Dyer.
And, yes, dry juniper wood burns almost
without smoke. Love, go to sleep. And dream
in juniper wood, in juniper fire.

from TOUCHING DOWN IN UTOPIA (2002)

THE OPENING

I imagine the 8 a.m. opening of the skipman's yard.
He is his mother's son and they are on the dot together.
His gates are unbolted, his skips ready, his crane yawning;
and his mother is looking up at him in the cab delivering
her last word. This might be an old photograph
in fifty years' time. Realism, turn-of-the-century, quaint:
'The Skipman's mother bids her son farewell.' Skips? Mothers?
What were they? In the background are yesterday's skips,
undigested planks hanging out of their mouths. There are things
that have happened and things that are about to happen.
He is saying yes, yes he has been there before but he hasn't.
On board he has a skip inside a skip inside a skip.
Once he's gone, up the single leafless lane of the by-pass,
the skipman's mother goes inside to man the telephone.
Over the years she has taught herself to tie her own hands.

THE OUTSIDE WORLD

Funny the two locksmiths
should charge for services
plus travel plus VAT
precisely what I got
in the post this morning
for a few weeks' writing.

Locksmiths, big men. Their bodies
wobbled at how easily
they'd got from them to us:
our call, them downing tools
and powering over here.
They'd get the door to open.

First they drank tea. Then one,
a shuddering jaunty one,
went round outside. Through glass
we watched him coming at us
with a chisel – which he slid
and waggled till the door

springs open, stumbling limbs,
the world, the flesh, the weather
all cram through, a man
who cleans his car to music,
leaves, a drone of something,
viruses, an air

of solving, shadows, boosters,
evolution, fire-engines,
the light of day can't get
enough of us, want to be seen,
want to be listened to – plus
time of course, plus travel.

I paid the men by cheque,
same as I got for poems.

COWS

Your father, asks the gleaming man in the photograph,
how rich is he, how many cows does he tend?
His face is a landscape weathered by huge skies.
You say to him, my father tends no cows,
there are no cows at the house of my father.

My father is not a poor man, you explain to him.
He does not sleep on pavements like poor people do.
He has a tall house, he has a wife, he has children;
he has a car, he has two bicycles, he has a wheel-barrow.
All he needs is riches to fill his poems.

I see now, says the gleaming man, why your father
has allowed you to come here to tend to us.
He is a rich man but he has no cows for his poems;
he cannot beg for food, he cannot sleep on pavements,
he hardly knows how to tremble under the sky.

He sends you, Dr Elinor, with your passion and your
education.
This I can understand: you bring us good healing
and you take home sad sentences of our country,
of war, of hunger, of the disease that squats in the spleen,
the disease that eats at our throats.

For here in Sudan no poem ever goes hungry.
No poem sleeps on the pavements of cities.
We are fierce here with the shortness of lives
and the endlessness of sky and land and sky.
And the rich men amongst us, they have cows.

OPEN HUT

The A.A. answered from Northumberland.
Pronounced my name as Mooah,
Mr. Mooah, which they said was right.
It must have come up on their screen
in Newcastle as here in Kent
I finished saying my policy.

No, not locked, and not a garage
(garage to rhyme with Raj), more a hut.
A hut? He thought about it.
I waited in his head and listened
to the raucity he'd hardly known (known
to rhyme with mourn) – clangs, screeches,
hootings, weldings, wrenchings in their
eerie absence, then, all round his head,
Motor Insurance, the balloon of them,
their brightly painted talk, their gas
burning away our distance.

You're joking, someone warm was saying
to someone easy at a chattering screen.
Mr. Mooah, don't you lock your hut?
I said a lorry backing down the lane
had knocked the doors off (doors
pronounced like cause). So this hut's
open-ended, let alone it's leaking.

Mr. Mooah, you'll have to put two pounds
on your premium. A pound
for every garage-door I didn't have.

I told him I'd be using Mastercard.

TOUCHING DOWN IN UTOPIA

1

We are flying at 20,000 feet, the pilot says.
He says Ethiopia very fast and leaves out the H.

Cake is served, and clingfilmed cheese buns. Underneath us
God has left out his ridges and plateaux and gorges

to dry. It is not the rainy season in Utopia.
With the tips of our plane's little shadow we stroke

the smooth brown body of the land, its silky ears.
We are happy up here but the pilot says

we have to go down to earth. He is rabbiting
sternly now, it is government orders he says:

we must keep the blinds of our windows lowered,
we must not see this place we are boring down to,

and we must not ask why. Is there something here
too hot for us to contemplate? Or too awful?

Is it slums or guns that we're losing our lovely height to?
Blinds drawn, we feel down for the land which, when it comes,

when it arches its back and bumps us, bumps us and takes us,
isn't the sculptured thing we thought of, molten and cold,

but sizzles past us, scorches our knees, our knuckles,
whirls white-hot. We rage back briefly, then seem to taxi

quietly round to where I imagine a shabby
old customs shed awaits us. ET703 we are.

2

Hello pen, hello pen, hello pen.
Beautiful thin children flock to us
from the land, from the dust of the streets.
Hello pen, we have a few but mostly
we don't give them the dirt-cheap thing they want
and they're singing hello to.

We can't rise to flocking; or singing,
even at 4,000 feet, Hello beauty,
Hello friendliness to whites.

3

It's easy to tell the good people
from the bad in these old paintings:
the good look out unswervingly,
two-eyed; the bad are seen in profile

as, this still-dark holy morning,
I see among the white-robed worshippers
your muleman of yesterday praying
just in front of me, to the right.
He's so close I could reach out and grip
his upper arm where he gripped you.

His profile's a wonder. I can't pray
like he can: I can look though, rub
my eyes with the half-face of the man
as priests here rub worshippers' bodies

with their crosses. From where I stand
he's lean-jawed, gleaming, aquiline;
he could do you traitors, anti-heroes,
stock pinched-with-envy usurpers.

Yesterday he took your upper arm
and saved you from falling. Back comes your
childhood in India, the ease,
the spreading bruise, pretty white girl
in the saddle, English girl, your old
houseboy at your elbow, the mountains
your icy sky. You notice ripped
plastic sandals as, to the twisting
dip and climb of the mule, your muleman
strings you along. On the way back
it happens: you lean from the shaly
precipice, lean and lean, and he
grips you, fights you, won't have you falling.

This morning your poor blood vessels
are a black ruin where he touched you
with his fierce fingers, his cross.

4

Early morning and we are climbing the mountain
before the day's brilliance cracks down on us.
We twist slowly up in the hill's black shadow.

The moon is a razor.

We meet stick-carriers, straw-carriers, grass-carriers;
and a young girl, bare-footed, light-footed,
on her way down the mountain to school.

Hello, she cries. Where are you go?
Each syllable clean as a bird-call, a prick of light.
The thin air cuts with her Rs.

5

This is the holy of holies
where the ark sits brooding.
Thick with sweet smoke a curtain
hangs between it and us.

Us includes us and the black
beseeching eyes of our trusty
deaf-and-dumb shoe-minder,
whose shoes have open soles.

This cruciform window too
is holy; it is both
early Christian and Muslim
in style. At the throat of it

there's a warm crossbeam,
a lively mid-morning
congregation of dust particles.
They can't sit still, these motes: vague

loopers of loops, goers, darters,
the crabwise, the shoeless, the blind,
the frantic. We're all of us there,
our holy spirits I mean.

6

Outside the cave an old woman waiting for tourists.
You sit down near her. Bruises are her second
language and when she sees yours she reads it off pat.

The two of you are so tickled you share smile-wrinkles
and the brightness of yes: how a man goes off
leaving black grainy fingerprints on the white of your arm.

7

In the city two roads crossing themselves at a crossroads.

Hoot and go in the bottlenecks, along the soft shoulders.

Goats at the gravelly edge in a warm brown goat-scene.

The Atlas Hotel's Mr. Atlas flexing his orange uniform.

You in Utopia, assonant, off to buy pineapples.

Skips at the intersection, pickers thigh-deep in litter.

White shawls with bundles of sticks going somewhere or coming.

In the slow lane walkers sharing their ears with wing-mirrors.

Five on a bench, hip to hip, with something going between them.

8

The Ethiopian Airlines official
with his trim uniform and his wonky computer,
tall, precise, courteous,
can't check tickets without again and again
high-stepping back to his office,
wading along the conveyor-belt, upstream,
over our lumbering baggage.

TO A YOUNG ETHIOPIAN TB PATIENT

Fifteen-minute friend, you won't get this letter.
I've no name for you, nor address; and you've no need,
if you're ill or hungry, I guess, for awe-struck
letters of thanks. Thanks all the same for drawing
level that day, catching me up as you walked:
me on my dawdling mule, you taking whatever
happened to happen in the swing of your stride,
TB, treatment, this last twist up to the village.

From the house of your father it's eight hours' walk
through the mountains, you say, no road. A dry
trickle of path, I imagine, and you coming
mildly along for your jab, the stars bristling,
land-mass aching with age. Young
African man, I'm sitting comfortable here,
fair's fair, you could topple me onto these rocks
head-first, I'm sure my mule would co-operate.
But you don't. You don't even ask for money.
Going up together we talk mules, chances in life,
the distance you've had to come. Your continent
soars underneath us. Even with your illness,
you could walk the hindlegs off me and my mule.

When you move lightly ahead, I can't see myself
catching up with you.

AT THE BOTTLE BANK

Mid-afternoon and you bring to the bank
your tiny 125-gram marmite bottle.

I'm there before you
unloading my barrow of pleasures, my
Chardonnays, Cabernet Sauvignons, Muscadets, Riojas,
drink I never knew I drank.
Green after green I slip my clanging
confessions into the box, into such
a self-splintering orgy I hardly notice

you coming mildly along and popping
your small brown soul in, your widow's mite;
or the clink of it
falling amongst Mackesons, Murphys, Newcastle Browns.

Don't worry, they'll pick the pearl of you out
from those jaggedly grinning sinners.

What about me, though, my crashed soul convulsing
in everyone else's convulsions?
We crash together on this:
colour, fruitinesss, elegance, texture, tang,
every turn-of-the-century wino and dino
crushed to the cocktail
of us.

We're green, wherever green has got to;
good as good goes.

THE INNOCENTS
(figures in Troyes Cathedral by Béatrice Tabah)

I guessed you'd come in here, to pool
your silences and let them fill

with wonder if not prayer.
What poise you have, knees together

pressed to a single stem
of glued newspaper: I seem

to be the only one here who
still hedges his bets, still has two

feet on the ground rather
than one. Like stars you are,

tip-toeing up for your lift-off
to milky wherever above;

or tip-toeing down. Now you've no vaulted
heaven, the sky's indeed

the limit, your cathedral soars.
O single-minded perchers, learners

in unbelief, the tall silence,
you say, that stoops and listens

to us so intently, hears
only the thud of us? Your fierce

young eyes stare out at what there is,
hard places and betweenness.

Innocents, thou shalt not hold dear
anything beyond wonder.

THE SCREECH

From the bedroom window
I can see your three illnesses
skimming about on the pond.

Over the years, glandular fever,
arthritis, cancer: your kingfisher
is totally vigilant, screeches

at minnows, at the pond's plumage
skimming by underneath it,
at the blink of a window,

at you when you go too far
and slowly back up the garden path
after work, or go too near.

FULL CRY

You heard. And what did you do?

Unlike me up here on my saintly column,
getting my suffering in before suffering kicks,

you raged. Kicked
furniture, God's justice, God, the sculpted
legs of the table you've always sat at:
why should the best of people, why should she
(my best of people) get cancer?

Friend, I've mildness to spare.
Can I sit at your table and take that
blunt fury of yours – for me, I mean?
Let me be wonderfully angry you,
and you be St. Hubert.

You know the one?
Usually riding a horse or there's one there grazing.
Into calming, easing, stroking, making whole;
and with just your softness for animals.
Remember the heron, its trust, how it came
To St. Hubert with one leg curled and unusable?
And how he healed it and went

break-neck back from mildness, its
slung stone twanging off through the trees,
through the startled bristle of thickets, the flare of birds.
Beloved underlings trampled, this saint on horseback
can't not get again and again
to the last gasp:

magnificent antlered Christ
run to the ground,
your trembling spear at the point where the neck
meets the clavicle.

NIGHTINGALE

In May, I can still hear you saying,
nightingales sing in the light as well as the dark,
only the sweet din

of daylight drowns them
in warblers, woodpeckers, the lyrical,
the egocentric sleek, the upstart self,

so when life-after-death comes up,
lets rip, lets loose in gorgeous riot,
my ears are singing too, I can't tell

if it's there, and if it is, which
is the voice from the thicket
where you, brother, perhaps are perching,

and which is the brilliant
clamour of now.

TRACKING

for Diana, who spent her wartime childhood in the Himalayan foothills.

1   In the National Park

We are rumbling tenderly through the jungle.
Our heads wag to the leisurely rippling plod
of an elephant. We are all elephant ears.

Who calls? Out there, inside our heads,
a jungle creature, curiosity, is hiccupping.
Or is that fear? If so, we follow it.

Wounds ripping a tree-trunk, dung, flattened
warmth in a thicket: a breeze of alertness
blows through the gathering deer. Now pug-marks,

mud tigerishly sprung from. An ancient
cavernous murmur comes from inside our elephant.
'We are too airlee,' elephant man says.

2   Kingfishers

Over the years I've shown you
kingfishers and kingfishers:
brilliant blue disappearances;
reds coming upstream towards you;
the beaky self in profile,
bunched and grim. None of them
ever quite sticks: they whirr off,
just visiting, not quite yours.

Today though, in your foot-hills,
you show me the chocolate head
and the almost English blue wing-bar
of a Northern Indian kingfisher.
It sits composed in the tree for us,
the eye at rest, the wings folded.
Above it the road goes mildly
up and up your mountain.

3   On the Road

On the way up, on the winding hill road,
the dark surprised us, we surprised the dark.

There, round the corner, nestling the road's stored
warmth, were nightjars, two of them, three.

Speckled, angular: Great-eared possibly,
or Long-tailed. Caught in our headlights,

in sudden light from the head.
We braked. They struggled up. I saw your

childhood fluttering past me, sharp-winged,
warm from the road. We could have touched.

4 Nanda Devi

Absentee daughter,
scintilla of snow in the sky,
you still play hide-and-seek in the garden.

You hide and hide: in the dark,
in the mist, in the high clear-headed
clouds which are you all over.

At 25,000 feet
you tend to retire after breakfast.
Sunrise was all you needed –

till now, 56 years later,
when your lit smile comes through the pines
and amazes the garden.

5 The House

On the wide stone verandah of this solemn house
your undauntedness must have squatted,
looking out level-eyed

at a woodpecker drilling a tree-top,
at the icy glow of seventy-miles-off mountains,
at the future's sizzling haze.

You are waiting for a war to be ended,
and a man to saddle the pony
that takes you to the army children's school.

Behind you there is a cool dark interior.
Each day you come through these doors.
This house houses you.

6   The Creaking Swing

I think when the wireless
at last said the war with Japan was over,

you went
for a special celebratory swing in the garden.

The allies were flying their flags over Norton's Hotel.
You creaked

India, England; England, India; India, England,
your legs

kicking you
up and back, pride and servility, rich and poor.

You jumped, left it to swing on its own, came back
on a troopship.

You'd already
begun to be you. Your swing creaks in my ears.

HEAD-ON

That's not you I suppose
or some newness of yours,
that fly travelling
on the wrong side of the road
at roughly the level
of an upright cyclist's mouth?

Cough it back up? Or,
now its pedalling legs
are embedding themselves
like little black roots
in the solid wall
of the throat, swallow it?

O rank outsider,
rooter, radical gad,
I was just going home
(from home, admittedly),
if not open-minded
open-mouthed, when you came

slap into me. O fly,
meeting head-on like this
doubles the impact:
not just that hurtling speck,
your proactivity, but my
air-headed uprightness.

GENTLEMEN

Face to the wall
this good intelligent man
is stalls away from me:
off limits, round my eye's corner,
its puritanical right-angle.

Yet from where I'm facing
I catch the full pent-up up-
roariousness of his flow.

Is it goodness I hear
beating its porcelain drum?
Or is that frantic agenda
what intelligence has to do?

Too late to ask him now:
he's dried off, zipped and gone
while I'm still plucking up.

Goodness is easy, we can handle that.

But intelligence, sheer articulate
braininess fountaining forth,
how can we trust it?

How can we not trust it,
we gentlemen-dunces,
facing the wall point-blank?

TO THE GUIDE AT AGORREGI IRON-MILL, NORTHERN SPAIN

You have invented your beautiful arms for two purposes:
one's to delight us with Basqueness and brisk utter
exactitude; and the other, well, with the side of the hand
you drop a perpendicular deluge (the horizontal's
your fore-arm rippling along to the other); or grind,
anticlockwise and clockwise, the tips of your fingers
against the tips of your fingers; or throw up
handfuls of sparks over your shoulders (I can see
kindling matted and black in furnaces
under your arms).

Not to mention your language –
Spanish or Basque or a mixture spinning your wheels,
the bellows fanning your fire, your trip-hammer tongue
going hell for leather, hell for impurities
(surrender, half-heartedness, compromise, all are impure),
the same stream, down through the oaks and apples, across
the top of the mill, the same old eighteenth century water
for both, turning and turning, everything's two,
working the rod white-hot and the grain golden,
smelting and grinding, chisels and dignity, sudden
explosions and bread-flour, land and the language.

CAT SENTIMENT

I find you on your last morning
staring across your territory.

You look furious or just fierce,
I can't decide which. Either way

you haven't a word for it. Or for
cancer or death or the dreadful

white flare on your chest X-Ray.
If only I could stare with you.

Share your wordlessness. Savour,
through cocked electric ears, the

suddenness of birds. Or fill
almond eyes with the lovely hover

of dots that is our territory.
You howled for this place, strutted

rigid for it; now you come
head-butting back and insist

on pouring the sweet squeezed juice
of your purr into my ear.

Rhythmic; drenching. So, friend, you
with the velvet head, I must learn

cat sentiment, must I? Sweetness
and fear and want. No words though.

MURMUR

Of garden citizens
preening the lawn of themselves;
or, deep in the church of the ear,
the remorseless throb of a hymn.

Mine, and I can't quite catch it.

"Once heard never forgotten,"
the consultant says
to forty would-be heart specialists
on the cardiology course.

From my curtained cubicle I hear them,
voices from India, Africa, Newcastle:
"Can I listen to your heart sir?"

Plugged, heads cocked for the blood-count,
they might be my grandchildren
goggle-eyed
at what we did in the old days.
They peer down through the bars of my rib-cage.

It's on the tip of their tongues,
my personal rush of blood, its heave,
its rip-away swoosh.

But the consultant is appalled:
several candidates have evidently not heard it.
And it's a classic case.

Back they come, murmuring, apologetic,
into the celebrity's tent.
An Indian girl from Birmingham

presses her hand to my chest;
the lad from Newcastle takes what's available
between my ribs: I
squeeze in a young Pakistani
next to my breast-bone.

All of them have been told
to hear my extraordinary murmur.
I might be a dying breed.

Male Standard English Class W-
hite.
Male Standard English Class W-
hite.

The throb of it in their heads.

"It's not so much a murmur,"
the consultant says to the candidates,
"it's a rattle."

from BEAUTIFULLY KEPT THINGS (2003)

A sequence of 16 poems dedicated to the poet's children,

Alison, Hilary, Andrew and Elinor, whose mother, Diana

Moore, died on 20 October 2001.

4

For want of a nail I have come
on your immaculate bench-plane.
Swathed in the white of a hand-towel

you have kept it for a future
final smoothing over or off,
and although you have wiped the print

of your palm from its steel,
I can see you still planing,
still leaning into your finish.

Love, I'm down to unfurling
tiny curled-up scrolls of you.

6

I have put your trekking sticks
in the corner reserved for sticks:

someone's hockey stick, a golfing
umbrella that isn't remotely
ours, and your NHS walking stick
you died too quickly to lean on.

Your trekking sticks though, they'll serve.
Easy-to-click, retractable –
I forget which briefcase you took
but they'll bed down nicely
with your pens, your notes, your language,
your pointy extendable mind.

I'll keep them for now in their corner,
to go – you must go, my love,
when you have to –
stilting off
over long cloud-like hills
or hill-like clouds.

8

There wasn't a warning, only
your voice from the green summer chair

arguing, laughing, drifting upwards
to lodge in the trees like mistletoe.

What's it to do now you're dead, now
your summer chair has been folded?

All winter, with the optimist ear
in collusion, it's up there brooding.

Comes back, I trust: as the clatter
of blackbirds, as tart green song.

9

To rise to every horror, every
everyday tragedy, the whole of it,
from the casual seed to the husk,
would be, George Eliot writes,
too much for us, like hearing
each individual blade of grass
growing.

Apparently, with eight months
now unlived, you stop the car
inside the gate of a hopfield.
It's late May. If everyone's quiet,
you say, they will actually hear
the ache of growing, of young hops
wrenching upwards, rising. 'Perhaps,'
Eliot says, 'our frames could hardly
bear much of it.' But you insist
on the whole of it. Everything
holds its breath.

Across the field the young
push back their roaring chairs
and stand for you, stand instead of you.

10

The quick-winged kingfisher
which last autumn gazed
so mournfully into the water
while every day you were dying

is gazing again this year.
I'm not sure what I'm fishing for.
Sympathy only? Morsels
to keep me swooping? Or the small fry

of grief that I still need
squirming beneath me. You go,
then my grief for you goes,
then what? Then I find,

in clear lifeless water,
your list of medicines you took
at exactly what time
of which last day, last night.

11

You saved your notes and kept them
in the bottom right-hand corner
of your computer screen's multi-
coloured possibilities.

I can't get in.

I click on the window a bit
where I might just find
the scented essence of you
here at your desk.

'Saved notes' you call them. I hope,
don't hope at all, they crackle
out in front of me and there's
your mind, your open-heartedness.

I'll do the saving now:
make you a file, type
the name of your soul, your password,
even press Enter for you.

12

You left your sandals behind, did you know? –
the ones I bought at 'Travelling Light'
two years ago now.

Narrow fittings you wore
but in these you could tread heavy,
be your ordinary foot-slogging self.

What I like is the broad
palm of their hands, and the fingers
meeting across your toes and half-way
up your feet and around your ankles.

I suppose what happened
was that weightlessness flooded back,
fingers gripped you and lifted,
and you, lighter-footed suddenly,
lighter-headed and -hearted,

rose and left your sandals
empty and neat in their box.

Hover a little,
beautifully kept soul.

14

It's good things happen gradually.
For months we have dawdled together
through the woods at the outer
edge of your life. All the time

in the world has now nearly
been had. You lean down
to let the new blown head
of the first snowdrop of the first

year since you died hang on you,
hang on the back of your hand.
We are gradually happening,
head and body and soul.

16

Beloved, I have to tell you
your work is missing you most grievously
and not at all.

The abstract you never presented at Leeds
has had to learn your voice:
'Contradiction,' it sings to itself,
'the dynamo of change'.

Last night I came on you crying.
You were standing next to the yew tree.
Do you cry at night
for me to contradict you?

So you can change? So you can go?
Intrepid adversary,
fearful angel,
common or garden soul,

change comes down the path wide-armed
to take you in.

from THE HEARING ROOM
(2006)

TRANSLATION

Aujourd'hui
(There is always)

je suis très content
(a weir coming up.)

C'est agréable
(The green river)

de recevoir une personne
(streams downstream)

avec qui
(stops)

on peut
(then topples)

sympathiser.
(delightedly over.)

HOW TO LISTEN

With the ears of course, where
every story enters, spirals
in and away.

Not with the nose (though many
do listen that way). The trouble is
our bony convexities can't quite
forget the thought of themselves:
our pernickety nose, our fingers
making their point, our feet in the door.

Listen with the hollows of the body:
the ears, yes, and the eyes and the mouth
and, I recommend, the undersides
of the knees. Is the listener sitting?
Well, under the knees, unseen, concave,
a cradle, that's where the wild-eyed
stories will come, then, next day,
next month, or the next, let
slip, let spout out under the table,
what was done, where, how.

MUSIC

Music of tins
by someone like Vivaldi.
You take the wrappings off
and throw them in.

Each tin goes down the same,
goes bouncing empty down
the throat to be
recycled.

Each is a fragment
of a piece, I think, for mandolin
or lute; a phrase plucked
and repeated.

Don't expect a message.
The rhythm that you hear
is of a tin
which doesn't say it once had
rabbit-flavoured cat-food in it,
pilchards, chopped tomatoes, garden peas.

A poem would have loved all this
but tins are different.
They rattle off without nutrition
information, recommended recipes,
words.

Music's as clean as that.

ONION

On your first visit
to fond new widower me,
you brought a beautiful dark-red onion.

Onions don't mean a thing.
Their multi-layers aren't layers of memory
(the more you peel, the more tearful).

Onions are themselves.
Yours sits here on the table
broad-bottom heavy, a dark red globe of its own.

And yet how uxorious onions are
in a dish. They'll marry with anything,
steak, vegetables, cheese.

I must still have that recipe somewhere:
red onion and apple,
poems and the people who write them.

AT A LOSS

I am your grief. When I first
came to you, I had no words.
All I could utter was a sort
of roaring curse.

I came to stay of course.
I think you thought I'd howl myself
and go. You had language though,
I copied it

and made my howls articulate.
"Speak me," I learnt to say, "make
mention of me, mutter me
in your sleep." All

this you did for me but still
my rawness pleaded: "Thread me
through you, let me come between
your things and you."

Slipping you on I grew
a body where I watched my slow
wound raise its sides and inch towards
a healing. I

was something now, I'd occupy
the air, fill up a pocket of it,
have an edge, an end. I might be
your live-in lover

the way you mind me, hoover
round the space you know I need.
Trust me, dear griever, I'm complete
and commonplace,

I promise.

FOR MACK MEHRABIAN, BAKER

When I told you about my wife,
you gave me a loaf,
straight off,

out of the crate
you were carrying, out of what
must be your fullness of heart, a state

of constant readiness,
blood always coursing, I guess,
always on the *qui vive* – in case

someone perhaps whose wife is dead
comes by, whose crying need
is for bread

or for something that's risen or rises.

APPROACHING READING

'This train will surely be arriving
at Reading.' And we've been moving

so sweetly along our line,
so single-mindedly. Acton

glided past as though it had
to happen, then Slough, then Maidenhead:

Reading we thought a natural
consummation, until

this First Great Western man
loudspoke himself uncertain.

Without at least a glottal stop,
God might have given up:

no signalling system, no word,
no getting anywhere.

AT THE CRICKET

Kent are playing Lancashire today.
We are interested to see what happens.

My neighbour says it's thick as shit, the atmosphere.
He says, You watch, it'll swing a mile.

A train goes by beyond the rhododendrons.
It gives two hoots. Quite near us
a lithe West Indian is deep third man.

We're clustered round a green arena
in a sort of dip. Which must be why
the pleasant summer haze
hangs on and on. It can't get out
and we can't not inhale it.

You should hear our clapping: how,
all round the ground, when someone hurls or hits,
we crackle up. Nothing actually catches,
but what if it did?

If the mist cleared and mild-mannered them
rose up and turned on mild-mannered us?
Decent us came out against decent them?

Left versus right I mean,
not Kent vs. Lancashire at all.

It's thick as shit, the atmosphere.
It will swing a mile.

I.D.

A passport will do. Otherwise
all they need is a modest
collection of poems, title and name
on the front, and a face-only
photo of the author himself
looking poetic on the back.

You get through the gate and they frisk you,
strip each poem from the page
and make it stand with its arms out.
They finger the ribbed cage of the lines,
count syllables, check for a rhyme-scheme
strapped to the calf or thigh.

OK, they sigh in the end. Yet again
they've found nothing, certainly not
anger, the small explosive
you flatter yourself you concealed
at the time of writing – to go
decorously off in the white

silences between stanzas.

IN THE HEARING ROOM

"There were rebels, you say,
sleeping in the house of your father?"

At the first kick
you hear the cheap timber gasp.

Gendarmerie, guards, officers, enterers, wrenchers.

Even the adjudicator is amongst the men
at the door of your father's house.

The adjudicator is perfectly dressed, perfectly spoken.
You long to please him, tell him the story he wants.
But you can't say. Fear has damaged your head.
Or shame. Or the breaking door.

So how come the man at the back of the court
swells with rebels
sleeping at the house of your father?

He brings them tea, eggs, oranges;
he watches them eat.

AT THE HOUSE OF MY FATHER

1

In the dim-lit attic dormitory
my father goes from bed to bed,
rebel to rebel. He has dragged up
every cushion, every rug in the house.

These boys are second sons to him.
He tweaks their soft ideals, their tufts,
their downiness; wishes them
good sleep, the sleep of men unwanted.

They drop their limbs like clothes:
take what's on offer
while, through the blur of breathing,
their ears' devices brim with news from the dark.

Last thing, as though I were all rebels,
my father's face leans down and kisses
my smooth one. All evening I've scoured
the rebels' pans with something as prickly.

2

Mornings I work in the washroom.
Before hanging I put
the rebels' clothes through the mangle.

They come from the sink drowned:
slumped shirts with their arms in the legs
of slumped trousers.

I ease them back into shape,
stretch out the arms in innocence,
make a V of the trousers.

Then, as I put them through,
I watch the men's cold fear
sluicing out down the runnels.

3

The rebels have one bicycle
between the lot of them.
It has flat tyres and the chain
is a dangling necklace.

But might
rebels not need a bicycle
to ghost off into the night
no one knows where (not
till it comes home pedals in shreds,
spokes gone, arms twisted)?

I can do punctures: hold
the breath under water, wait
for the gash in the inner tube
to show me the place, to come
trumpeting up in bubbles.

I can do chains: upside-down
hand-pedal inches forward
till the racked links take,
the cogs remember.

At the back of my father's house,
the gaunt frame drums its wheels
for when a ghost might need it.

4

The men found our old kettle
from before the regime.
After that there was no holding them:

our two benches in front of the stove,
they sit inside themselves
and hear in the distance the first

mew and tick of spirits about
to rise, then, in the whisperings
as the chest and shoulders fill,

their sense of justice
wheezes, courage croaks,
purpose breathes up the spout.

5

Over the rebels' heads,
on my father's rooftop,
I spend clogged grey evenings
sending my pigeons out
on their rounds and calling them.

The hatch clatters back.
Rebels are nothing now, only
a thud of cards; sometimes,

when one of them plays his ace,
a rumble up of men,

a beat of wings. Once
out of their cage, the pigeons
gust free as the thick
air unlocks and lets them
go swirling through it.

The men don't know but they gave
my pigeons their names.
I keep them just under the breath:
no pigeon is mentioned by name
when I call them home.

NOTICE OF ARRIVAL

I am shut in the hold of my head.
It's so dark I'm bodiless
yet I blunder about and bruise
on the luggage I'm stacked with,
memories, fear, loss.

The drivers are up on deck.
For the moment this juggernaut's mine.
We have come all the way together,
its roaring shudder and the shudder
of my muteness. As for its snore
I know it like it must know
the cry, the nakedness of my waking.
Perhaps it can feel at the back of the neck
me wafting amongst its freight.

I'm becoming more pointed, I think, more
ship-shaped as we cross. I'm the tip
of the iceberg, I know, tapered, stream-lined
for parting the water. I can picture
the thin frothed-up wake I leave behind me;

and how hugely we're nosing in
between harbour walls. I have to get
back now into my limbs, re-enter
my rib-cage, put on the empty boots
of my legs, and my old voice-trumpet.

One thing I have decided: when I come,
I shall come clean, quite openly tell them
that I'm almost nobody.

ON THE BORDER PATH

I take you along this gentle path between counties,
Kent, as it happens, and Sussex. Way
above us and utterly white on blue,
the clouds are a picture: Truth and Justice and Mercy.

Quick, wary, in unsuitably shiny shoes,
you're pleased, I'm sure, this isn't Iran we're skirting;
not quite at ease, though, in all this rolling mildness,
this rich, lucky, carefully planted space.

'There are even now mines in these fields?'
I walk alongside you at the very edge.
In the staccato of your almost excellent English
I can't not hear the quake in the hills of your head:

the border erupting, the grassy lid of it
lifted from under your feet, under your shiny shoes.

PICNIC

You remember our seaside picnic,
what a storm we ran into?
And how we were all flinging wildly,
swatting out of or through.

I was afraid that my white
was what thunder-flies dream of.
But your stripes were the same,
black-spattered, a bug-hive.

Odd you should swat your way
from Zaire to find that asylum
is picking specks off a cold meat pie,
then off strawberries and cream.

We didn't get stung – that was good,
but the best of the picnic was this:
how mildly discomfort thundered,
wanted to be with us, touch us;

and, even more, how it didn't care
that you'd had to flee from torture
and I had not. Here's to discomfort,
its indiscriminate spatter.

DREAM WARFARE

I think torturers don't so much dream
as make sudden dream appearances,
and the terrible tapes unwind night after night
in Toronto and Stockholm and Birmingham.
You'd think they'd be curious to watch them.
They're asleep, though, far too busy
doing smile-shots, boot-shots, raised-arm-shots.
Him and him and her they leave to their dreaming.

This one, startled at 3 a.m. to breathless
alert, can't doze. How can he dream
sweetly? Even here where he's fled to,
their broadly tormenting smile comes up the street
towards him. He goes the long way round
these days or darts into sleep and dreams
suddenly, when there's nobody there.

LOCKED

You can forgive, you say,
the man who beat your feet,
who hung you up by your hands,
who drove you past pain's limit.

The man you can't forgive
tortured next door, next cell:
beat your friend, hung your friend
by the hands, made your friend howl.

Your cries lay down with you,
touching, coaxing, whispering.
Your friend's cries are locked
in the cell of your hearing.

from THE BURNING HOUSE

1   Case

On the map of your case for asylum
there's a small hole in the page
where your home village was.

Then there's your first arrest.
Holes are deeper here, more jagged:
they made you strip, they assaulted you.

After that there's a gap: three
empty years when you looked after cows
and the flesh is whole, unopened.

From there a broken bottle
has printed the route you took on your thigh:
Darfur, Khartoum, London.

3   During sun and rain

Your long sky ended here,
deep in the midlands of England.

Asylum's a green wind
that sings in Her Majesty's corridor.

You clap big farmer's hands
silently together.

5   In the telling

When words fail
or the voice fails words
that need to be said and accepted,
your left hand goes on speaking,

flicking open and closed
as though you're not so much scattering
grain as throwing it away
on land you've had to abandon.

Your voice can't say what was done,
what the young men did when they came.
Atrocity you have to say
left-handed.

6   The burning house

As though this
was the morning after,
we visit you in prison and view
the burning house of you.

Janjaweed keep coming:
blackening the houses, then,
when you're building back,
bristling round you and cramming you

over and over
into the back of their car,
hilarious even now your gasp
when they stub your flesh with burn-holes.

Bad sleeping, you say.
Smoke grieves in the timbers,
breathes from the black of the house.
Startles back into fire.

from WHISTLING BACK (2012)

BACK-TO-FRONT

> 'I have tried to resolve this difficulty by slightly prioritizing the reader who wants to read from front to back.'
>
> Mark Rowe, *Philip Larkin: Art and Self.*

Is it that we are lazy,
we slightly unprioritized
beginners at the end, readers from Z

to A? It's not we read
books backwards or left-eyed.
It's not we're only interested

in leaping to a book's
conclusion, looking
in on things and people when they're locked

to what has happened. Or
is it we like to enter
at the moment, now, when 'there'

turns into 'here'? Front-
to-back is different:
greedy for precedent,

front-to-backers like footprints
they can follow, an argument
where the current

floats them forward or a story
leading them through doors
(all this in the past, of course).

SIGHT-READING

I like to see the cricket scores.
Not too much, not commentaries or pictures.
Only totals, what each player

made or took. Going backward
from the bare thing that occurred,
that's what I like: letting words

trail behind and be the ghosts that write
their drift of afterthoughts
in place of sounds and sights.

All you need is the score. Then
you can hum the tune
to yourself and have it playing on

and on in your head while you
don't listen to it or you do.

BAREFOOT
*Version of a poem by Lotfollah Pour Abdullah,
translated from Farsi by Nasrin Parvaz*

You exist. I love you.
I love you for your dear existence,
not for being mine. What I love
is all and that you are.

I praise you and I praise
your search for yourself: you walking
barefoot through fire to prove
your trust in men's trustworthiness.

Handcuffed, barefoot still, you leaned that day
against the stone wall of the Justice
Prosecutor's office. Kindness
smeared your eyes. You smiled it whole, unwrinkled.

Life, fear, death that day were different, true
to their first definitions. Hope had a shape
like a limb you could stretch forward
to touch and it touched you back.

And the price for such blind believing?
The price to pay for using the seven mild letters
of the name for torture – Trust Open-
handedness the Right to Think Unorthodox
Resistance Energy – was torture.

Believe even now, dear son,
the night-sky of your love has stars
which shine with waiting.

One should live twice: once
to learn to live and once to live.

DIU
for Tim Malanga

'Diu,' our Latin teacher told us,
meant 'for a long time'.
Once learnt never forgotten
('too long,' you said in your letter).

We never questioned him,
never thought to ask how long
a long time ('too long
without working, too long fearing')

was – whether 'diu' was like
the steep twisting path ('deportation,
too long feeling uncertain, too long
living on £34 a week')

up through the trees to the black ridge
at the top, precipitous place
('too long crying, too long
being asked'), beyond which

long was too long, 'diu'
('at a reporting centre') had no
more meaning; and joy,
excitement, they must have dropped through

a hole in the world, a crevasse.
Too long, too long. Once learnt
never unlearnt ('to confirm
my name, my address').

FISHMONGER
for Simon the fish

A fishmonger I know
delights in Seamus Heaney's poetry.
What makes him happiest though

is when the rugby team he supports
beats its opponents
haltingly, is only fluent in parts.

Then he senses there's a feast
in the making, when nothing
is overcooked, nothing is forced,

and well-oiled everything comes off.
I've seen him stowing unsold
fish in his fridge and wonder if

as a fishmonger he
has days when, yes, he wins but only
just and unconvincingly,

and if tonight he's going home
to sumptuousness: an open
book, a Seamus Heaney poem.

NICETY

Cock pheasant, plump and brilliant,
how did you know
the need, precisely now,
to glide down
into my friend's garden
and with fastidious steps
tip-toe across it?

Were you perhaps
in mid-laborious flight
distracted, oddly drawn
down? I don't mean
the claws of a sparrow-hawk
spurred you into such promptness,
I don't mean gunshots.

It's just I think necessity
isn't always dire. Not
if it's kind enough,
precisely now,
to send plumpness and brilliance
high-stepping across flower-beds,
let alone hope.

DIMENSION OF THE SOUL

'Hope is a dimension of the soul…not the conviction that something will turn out well, but the certainty that something makes sense, regardless of how it turns out.' – Vaclav Havel

We stopped at the end of the street
to post a letter and the car-keys
got involved: hopped out and down
through iron bars into a drain.

Have to admit, we did hope
we could heave the drain-top
off: go down head-first, fishing
about in leaf-sludge to bring

our precious keys up. But the bars
weren't falling for that, they were far
too heavy, so we had to abandon
the thought that miracles happen

lift off just like that – and look
for a sensible stick to poke
between and down, and hook through
what was there. After all, you

rarely see a bar without
barlessness either side of it.

VOICE-OVER

Poor you,
you haven't heard a cuckoo
all spring, you say,
and already it's late May.

Back here
the two utterly mellow syllables
are everywhere,
they've colonized our thoughts.

Is what
keeps sweetly repeating
at or in or through us
a bird of the woods or the head?

I know, why
don't I open the window
and offer the phone to the woods?
They'll put you through.

You'd hear
the rustling heart murmur of trees,
you'd hear the insects' roar,
you'd hear the cuckoo.

Like hearing
some long silent part of yourself
call to you through the blur
and you saying yes to it.

TAKING THE VOW

The marriage vow I take,
to go on doing things
happily with you for ever
(if 'ever' is another
word for 'now'),

flows through its valley,
glints, seems never
not to have flowed precisely
here (if 'never' is a word for
'not for quite a time').

We must have come down from the ridge
through woods, through meadows
and found this vow
winding its way (if 'our'
is what we mean by 'its')

along the river-bed
that all these meadows slope to.
My vow's a natural,
saying nearly nothing (if
'nothing' is a word

for river-whispers,
watery murmurs of approval
that what the hills and trees and fields
have long suggested
is being said).

BAT MUSIC

The concert has barely begun
when a chip flies off
the already-quite-old block
of music the band is playing.

The trumpet is scorching
the roof-beams and wall
to wall a hectic
something is jagging about
in the saxophone's breath and trombone's
upward pourings.

Not often you actually see
off-beat fragments
rocketing round
in the empty space of a church.

Not often the holy ghost
comes down from its roost
and you see how frantic it is,
how distressed.

NO HANDS

Which came first,
time or the face of the clock?
Detainees or the grim wired block
where detainees are detained?

Did the blank clock-face
keeping the young men's hours
to itself (its hands are gone;
gone, I guess, for repairs)

come first?
Or timelessness, indefinite
detention, the hours of the night
and then the hours of the day?

QUAIL
for Nasrin Parvaz

My neighbour keeps a quail
inside a shed (in solitary

confinement in Iran
you used to tap out messages

on your next-cell neighbour's
wall). We're left alone

for hours, this quail and I,
caged up, well, I'm fenced off

(and wait for a response), and so
it's no surprise that when

it whistles out its call
(you're never sure, you said,

your next-cell prisoner
might be planted there to

listen, to entice), I whistle
back to it in Quail

as nearly as I can:
the little stutter, then

the full-blown upward-tilting
hoot. I hoot quite well,

I even know the Quail
for 'solitary' and 'I'.

I BELIEVE

In what? In miracles
I guess: in whatever
drips or trickles

through and fills a paving-
stone or sparrow-hawk
or loving

with stuff it needs to be
another thing as
well, entirely.

RING
for Udo Adam-Pasquale

The silver ring
a calm, most dear, unshowy man
has made for me

I flash (surprisingly
to me) around a bit, although
of course it's private, a

revolving carapace
of brilliant hits, of little
hammered facets

beneath which no one
sees. If I could write
as aptly, expertly

as he's hammered (no
first person, no precious
stone inset) I'd

enter for some
prize-prestigious showy
competition a poem

so calm, so intimate, so
easy to slip on,
it slips through unselected.

from THE BRIGHT GAZE OF THE DISORIENTED (2014)

BOY'S NAME

The wooden post in the pond
where the kingfisher perches
is a bare post, and indeed
when they asked you your name
you couldn't say anything.

You knew it of course. You'd answer
if somebody said it. Kingfishers
come back, they don't abandon
their ponds. Look, it's there
staring into the water.

You lost everything, home, family,
country. How did you bring
that totally warm smile
through immigration? Or did it come in
hanging under a lorry?

So much is closed down now,
barricaded on the narrow streets
of your memory. It would be good
if, in its quite un-English plumage,
there on its post was the kingfisher.

But it's not. There's only a post. Enough
that your lost name – its kingfisher
colours I still can't really pronounce –
flits between blackened houses
and comes laughing back to you.

AFGHAN IN LONDON
for Stephanie

Sleep longs for him.
It leaves its door wide open.
It waits for him in his favourite places.

But he rides past.
Can't glance, can't even think the live-wire
thing he knows, the live-wire thing that knows him.

All night
his bicycle whirls him on, whips
the spinning top of him to a pitch

too high-screaming
to hear the men when they came
to his father's house. The men when they come.

MISSED CALL
for Jane

You phoned just after you hadn't quite
seen an osprey. Your friend saw it. You
went back to the car and while you were gone

a small white hovering Christ must have come,
its claws demurely tucked and a harness
across its shoulders of huge dark wings.

I've not seen ospreys either. Which is good –
good for hoping, I mean, good for believing.
Please phone, love, when you miss an osprey again.

MURMURATION FOR EDDIE

Was it that white-skyed, black-skyed
Friday evening we saw
the spectacular Mexican wave
starlings do before roosting
when you Eddie?

Hundreds, maybe a thousand
black leaves in a leafless tree,
multi-twittering, multi-chattering, then,
as if on command, a single
silent voice. While you Eddie. While we

gaped at the smoke of them
gusting across the valley, one plume
of bird, wafting, swirling, twisting.
While you Eddie in your top-floor flat,
single-minded now in the last of the light.

Were they taunting, only
Seeming to leave? Scatter of grit
thrown off, then whirling upward and round
and back, into their plumages, burnt
black on the cold white of the sky.

One smoke-in-the-wind thing,
starlings that Friday evening when
multi-talented you Eddie,
multi-active, multi-spirited, multi-caring,
ended your single life. No use

asking why, what wired these brains
to their act. You're gone and we,
however adept we are at not
missing each other too grievously,
miss you Eddie, miss you.

TO THE MAN WHO PICKED MY POCKET ON THE 149

Dear thieving man,
I guess in the blur of all your split-
second snatchings you don't remember me,
once you'd spotted my pocket, I mean,
and the tip of the brown leather wallet
inside it, not quite snugly.

Let me remind you.
You got on the 149 at Dalston Junction.
Perhaps it's your patch, perhaps you always do.
My stop would be Shacklewell Lane.
I turned to the window to look.
You couldn't believe your luck.

Five or six times since then
I've used you, stolen you for my story:
how the bus stopped, drawing open
its doors for you; the crash of your exit;
you side-stepping through shoppers; my pocket
inside-out and empty.

So, thieving man, we're accomplices,
you and I. I start again and again
at Dalston Junction. You do too – how,
in broad daylight, this man
on the bus was staring out of the window,
pocketing people's stories.

TO AN INTERPRETER FROM A COUNTRY AT WAR

Beating, burning, killing:
you know the men's stories

almost before they tell them.
Tender-to-hear home-language

comes to your door in London,
the hearing room of your head.

English equivalents, they're
no problem. Translation, though,

is an echo that howls back,
loudspeaks grief of your own.

THE ULTIMATE RENDITION

is
to find a word
of quiet dignity, impeccably
connected (music, literature),
that will ask no questions
and will stop at nothing
(not the sending

of a man
by plane across a sea
to somewhere else, so somewhere else
can torture him and we don't have to)

and make it seem
a mild necessity, it happens,
it's rendition,

like the sea's gesticulations,
wrenching, heaving upward
as the plane comes over,

like dread
that trickles coldly down the spine,

like handcuff-sores, like sobs.

KRAMM'S IAMBICS

Did the bell ring? Did we call to him?
I can't remember. What I hear
and hear is the rhythmical bounce
of Revd. Heinz Herbert Kramm
down the stairs from his attic bedroom
to an English wartime supper.

Two steps, one light, one thuddingly
accented taking the Pastor's
weight; then two steps more, ker-
Kramm, two more, two more. These were
my first iambics, first refugee,
first person from Germany.

What did my father and mother mean
taking him in, feeding him,
letting him not wash up? *I must
jump away*, he said when he'd finished
his food, and they let him.

We tried our best, my brother and I,
for the allies, for us. What
we wanted was victory, wasn't it,
total dominance. We filled
his bicycle bell with gravel,
air gushed from his tyres.

Iambics, though, have lodged in my head
ever since: the thud, the thud, the thud
of coming downstairs to join us,
of nothing absolute, men being men,
enemies not being enemies.

SIGNING UP
for Lawrence Sail

I wanted to say
we've been friends for 52 years
and how good.

But the sea
doesn't count on its fingers of spume
the times it races up beaches.

And the land
makes no mention of blessings,
let alone issues annual statements.

So I didn't try.
I'd have floundered, I'm sure,
out of my depth in sentiment.

What I did
was surf about in the shallows,
and when you signed with Avaaz
to stop the circumcision of women,

I signed too.
Did you see me there, four seconds behind you?

FOOTSTEPS
for Elinor

Waiting for news, for a blessed call
to say my child, her mother's
daughter still, is now
a mother herself,
I might as well

watch blackbirds
hopping weightlessly across
the bristle of my new-mown grass,
three or four hops, stop,
three or four more, toward

the grandmother
of all twisted willow-trees,
who, though she seems too gnarled to care,
spins round to catch them at it.
They freeze, just happen to be there.

IN PRAISE OF ROWING

You square your oars
and push the flat of them
flat through the dense
coherency of water.

You drive each oar's-worth
spinning back towards
the time you first dipped in
too deep, too splashily.

You get the rhythm
and you do this simple
cursive thing. You can't
of course look forward,

follow some fixed intention
marked up on your
horizon. All you can do
is gaze the length

of all the froth behind you,
re-read it as it settles.
Where can you go
but on from what you've written?

HOSING DOWN

You might be lucky. You might
be on the 17.24 from Waterloo
to Charing Cross and happen
to be glancing left precisely when
a gap between two buildings
rumbles past with two hard-hatted
men in it, also a mixer
which has finished mixing, a
crusted wheelbarrow and spades.

This can't be willed of course.
It's pure luck if, as you pass,
it happens one hard-hatted man
is at that moment hosing
clean the other's wellington
boots. Don't miss the care he gives,
the way he stoops and comes
in at an angle and the other
lets him do it, trusts him.

Trains come past any minute here
especially at rush hour, the time
for slowly stopping work. You
might be lucky if you took
the 17.21 or 17.28 and happened
to glance left and see the other,
in a gap of what seems happiness
between before and after,
hosing the first one's boots.

HERON ENDING

When what seems like an ending
comes to you, when you find

yourself standing on the far
side of some sort of water

glaring back at it, when there's no
question of spearing any more

fish, you grapple up, your front
as always too heavy. You beat

stiffly off. Nothing remains
to be left fiercely unsaid.

from THE TREE LINE (2017)

THE TREE LINE
after a painting by Haymanot Tesfa

If people were trees, your painting
seems to say, then whatever
colour they were (there's green, there's brown,
there's shocking pink, then black,
white, orange, yellow, green again),
they'd stand, their arms slung open
round the shoulders next to them,
their heads, their roughly textured
growths of coloured foliage,
not just lending ears to each other
but jaws, cheek-bones, temples, nerves of the face.

Your line of trees shines out against
a blue-green blur of night. Roots
locked, knuckled to a ridge
of upturned stony soil,
I think they are facing grief together
or a firing-squad. All I know
is if one of them had its trunk
shot away, two others would hold
its head entwined with theirs, taking
its pain, feeding its story's hunger,
doing its living instead of it.

ARRIVALS

In spite of all
the usual warnings poems give, delayed,
expected, landed, now unloading, you

out of the multi-national altogether mix
who used Arrivals on the day we did
chose me,

burst out of Short Term Parking through a
knot of people holding other people's names up,
partners

dropping everything to be together, to where
outside a café I was watching never
having met you

for someone known and wandering and dear
I hadn't thought to buy a bunch
of roses for.

The flowers were pink and almost scented.
Their stems leaked puddles on the table-top,
which wasn't much

to pay for being
arrived at so whole-heartedly, even
short-term trusted while you fetched

your coffee
and whoever you would give the roses to
was queuing at Passports, Customs, Immigration
to be cleared for you.

ON THE ROAD TO LE BLANC

You don't remember, do you,
the way the steps of the church
at Nouans les Fontaines
drop steeply almost into the road?
Why should you? We never stopped
At Nouans, never looked inside.
You'd know the road though, D675,
through St. Aignan, where we camped
and swam in the Cher, through Nouans
and on, almost dead straight,
to Le Blanc. Every August
we'd take this road past the church
where, without us knowing,
while we swam, while we drove,
grievers, white-faced, the mother
white in the swirl of her hood and gown,
are gazing down at the dead
body of Jesus. I have to tell you
yesterday I took the road again.
It's April here on earth. D675
is lined with cowslips, white
with blackthorn, cherry, plum. Each tree
is fountaining its hazy prickle
of new leaves, wants to be seen,
wants to come out in a painting.
In Fouquet's fifteenth century *Pietà*
a man who looks like Jesus
with the same red hair is thinking
thoughts and holding back his tears.
It is the end, the new can't wait to start.

YOUR VOICE WHEN YOU SING
for Haymanot Tesfa

Sometimes your voice when you sing
catches fire and I hear
the flames of it blazing,
licking up your tall
chimney of song.

Mostly I think of it
cutting a channel
through silence, which is
as it always is when you sing,
an ice-field suddenly
rigid, hardly daring
to breathe.

AT THE CAMP GATES

You say your grandfather
was one of the first British officials
to enter a Nazi Concentration Camp
at the end of World War Two.

It must be in the blood to care
for the detained. I've heard you
sleepless at night for men
with minds gouged out by fear,
by waiting without knowing
when or if. Your grandfather
will have opened the gates and seen
the shrunk chests and stomachs
and given all his care, the care
you give when here in Britain,
now, the gates of such a camp
inch open and a damaged
man emerges undetained.

FOR THE DETAINEE WELFARE GROUP WALKERS

I'm watching you dawdle
two-by-two on a path
through a field. Your slow
motion isn't, I can tell,
because you can't go fast
or you're dreading to come
to the end. You are taking
time, which is empty and yours
till you enter the wood. Walking
along you turn your upper
bodies (the trees as they wait
must be craning their necks
to know this) toward
one another, lending
your ears, your senses.
Then, when the field ends,
you come to a stile.
You queue to climb over it, in
through its seven locked doors.
The wood is thick with stories.

THE BELIEVING OF TREES

There's no need to finger
the wounds of the trees
to believe them.

You can trust
tell-tale scars, branch loss,
 uprootedness.

Even their stories
don't have to be true
to be true of them.

Stand in their presence.
Breathe in time with them.
Wait with them.

DIMINUENDO

Not at the end
of Tchaikovsky's Piano Trio
in A Minor but certainly
toward it

there's a trickle of glistening
sound which wets
the tongue of a rock and steals
over so

finely you ask, Can sound
rise from a pool
of silence and play
ever again

after that?
Or, after such exquisite
dying, can there be
life?

Or even, is there anything
left of death
after the moist of such
listening?

FALLEN TREE

What's left of it,
silver-skinned and riddled
with woodpecker holes,
lies in the grass, its head
propped on an elbow.
Seasons and seasons
of piercing blackbird song
have made its hollows
their home. I've not
been there but I think
listening may be the last
good thing most of us do.

CHANGE AT LEEDS

I can see you now.
You draw yourself up
to your full height, your best
South East English, to ask
a uniformed man at Leeds
about your connection to Bradford.

He shakes his head, tries
his Yorkshire accent on you.
You hardly catch a word.
Is it an exile's homing
instinct that you slip back
into sleep-talk and ask,

in Amharic, what platform
please for Bradford? And that
he, in sleep-talk too,
gives you platform number,
time of departure, arrival time
at Bradford, in Amharic?

FOR FIVE REFUGEES, ONE OF THEM A PIECE OF PAPER

I'm thinking that escape can't rest
until a journey back occurs, escaping
back. Ten years go past and then,
your citizenship, your passport
in your pocket, you take a boat
just like the one that carried you
across inside it (in a bin,
your head between your knees) and ride it,
stand on its deck like a mast.

And you and you and you, how
you must have cowered in the dark
hold of what they did to you,
their punching, entering, beating.
Somehow you stole off, coaxed that thing
up to a crack of light, allowed it
to have happened, spoke it, wrote it,
flew the fact of it as a flag in the wind.
You crossed back, you escaped.

And you, the ache for someone absent
written right-to-left on prison
notepaper, ten or twelve flimsy
lines, you slip out past the censoring
pens of guards at visiting-time.
Then, the scribble on the same
note's underside, you come back
escaping: the ache for someone else
who's absent, slipping back into prison.

RESISTANCE

A man is sitting waiting
for a spoonful of stiff honey

to obey the law that governs
honey when it hangs above

a bowl of porridge from a spoon
inverted. A sluggish dollop of it

gathers honey-weight and leans,
is torn from what stays clinging

to its spoon, which isn't much
to lick at, though its narrow

scrape of upside-down defiance
could by example teach a man

the sweet necessity of sticking,
standing stiffly up against.

SETTING THE TABLE
for Farkhondeh

We don't share much of course,
certainly not a language. And yet
with luck, with patience… Lucky
the decking for instance, pine
planks which gave us a platform
to bring out a table for lunch,
was slightly uneven. One of us
at each end, we lowered. Always
it wobbled, one leg wouldn't
touch ground or a plank had warped.
Until a steadiness suddenly
came, a perfect fit as if
we hadn't been looking for it
but patient, testing every surface
before trusting, it for us.

THE TULIP TREE
for Ahliyah

You can see how it might
have grown, the straightest way
from the root of the tree
to the sky, the trunk thick-set,
unbending (I imagine the great tree
your grandparents must have been,
upright like that), but the straight

way is blocked and the tree
has bowed to the bushy mass
of a fir, has ducked away
and found the sky elsewhere
(your grandmother lives on
in French, you speak it with her),
has branched, has multiplied,

has tulipped every summer (this
is your sixth, you speak Lingala
with your father, English
at school, Swahili, French
and English with your mother).
You reach for light, your tongue
leaps into flower.

from THE FEEDING-STATION (2019)

AT THE FEEDING-STATION
in memory of Steve Bovey

In your last long far too scarce
summer days you knew this scene
without looking: the darting
of bird after bird into open
garden where peanuts hang,
niger and sunflower seed.

Crossed threads re-crossed, bird-
lanes from hedge to feeding-station
and back, the map of it
you must have known by heart,
your struggling delightable heart.

Thought-lanes follow bird-lanes, dart
to wherever you went when you died
and back, beaks loaded,
woodpecker, blue tit, sparrow
and your beloved family
starting again on their lives.

I still don't know
if the dead come flitting back
to feed on the lives of the living.

The living though, left-alive
grieving ones, they're rich
in thought-lanes, story-lanes, voice-lanes.
They flit from the hedge to feed on you.

THE UNDERSTANDING

Strange to be watched
by a wren perhaps and a sparrow
while opening the door of the shed.

Like being watched by the dead
who must surely have seen
that the door hangs at an angle

and what you do to get in
is slip the toe of your boot
into the gap at the bottom

and raise it enough to unlatch.
You have to trust the dead,
that they know, that they're good,

as are the wren and the sparrow,
at keeping things understood.

ROUTE BARRÉE

Route Barrée, the barrier announced
leaving just enough space to pass.

Further down the road, hand-written
on a piece of cardboard, *Inondation*.

Later, more official warnings, black
on yellow, *Inondation, Inondation.*

The flood had drained away; what remained,
its level rising as it filled the valley,

was a wind and rain of people
with no places, of no address

but cardboard, plastic sacks, torn canvas.
Storm after storm of them had crossed

two continents and had unloaded here,
here where the route was barred.

BURNING DIARIES

Burning a person's diaries
smoke you make
goes straight up into sky
without a wobble of doubt.

Only at a gust or when
you think the diaries
were illegible anyway
does the smoke billow

like one of the writer's 's's.
Or more than billow –
come back, gesticulate, blow
stinging 'e's and 'f''s

in your eyes when you write
to yourself, *Writers really only
write for themselves*. In his diary
my grandfather called the day

his 15-year-old son died
the worst day of his life.
To match the pain? To lessen it?
Or in case, 90 years later,

his grandson might need a reminder?
That worst day went up
in the same smoke as the rest,
into sky, unswervingly.

AT LES ANDELYS

Like parents going not that
early off to bed, the sun
goes down, down river, down
the slope of day. What light
it leaves is thin smoke
hanging in windless air,
then not smoke at all. Long
after midnight, white cliffs
on one side chalky still,
a shape which might be forest
on the other, the river is
a curving silver bar.
Don't ask how it holds its light.
Upbringing I guess, what
goes shining on in you
without you knowing.

ALONGSIDE

Boats are good at this,
at coming up alongside
mooring-places, jetties, wharves.

Ways of thinking aren't
as navigable as boats.
Sometimes though it's possible

to bring them up alongside
other ways of thinking
and even in rough water

take supplies on board.

WALKING ALONG

A wish I have
is for my fellow walkers

to follow paths through woods,
up hills, along the banks of rivers

on both their legs, not hopping
on a single one but holding

two contradictory versions,
two possibilities, two stories

in one mind and going equally
along with both of them

as easily, as interchangeably
as when they kick one leg

ahead of them and trust the other
to come up from behind and pass it.

THE SLEEPING CHILD

I can see you now,
wonderfully still smiling,
telling a group of mentors
the young refugees they look after
aren't children at all, their
childhoods are spent already.
As you speak you are holding
a child asleep on your chest.

What did the mother mean
handing over her child?
Did she sense you needed
a sleeping child on your chest
to share breathing with, to share warmth?
Or to ease you from what
you witnessed, from having to smile,
from being unshockable you?

And the child, listening in,
one ear pressed to your ribs,
what did it hear so kind
it couldn't not sleep? Only
a sleeping child, I guess, can hear
the distant throb in a chest
of having been father once,
then not father at all.

WHAT THE STORY SAID

Friend, more than friend in the good
bad times when you told me, I

am your story. You remember?
You spoke me and I became

all that you'd been through, all
that was left of you, you.

Why did you leave me? Was I
too polished to live with,

my words too final, too solving
to be a solution when

it came to the fortnightly
summons to stand in a queue

and sign on, to coupons,
charity, life after telling?

BATHROOM TAPS

The taps
above our basin in a place we stayed
faced slightly inward
as though exchanging views
about our washing habits.
One of these taps
you twisted clockwise and water
spouted out and down as if
all future time was stacked up
in a reservoir
and couldn't wait to happen.

The other tap
you twisted anti-clockwise
back into the past.
You could feel the difference.
Anti-clockwise water
if you let it can remember
ancient lakes and what it's like
to be a cloud and making
dints in rivers and spattering
and people twisting clockwise
getting nowhere.

IN THE SIMPLE HALL
in memory of Eva Cohn

In the simple hall
we use for fund-raising events
there's a powerful electric hand-drier
just inside the toilets.
It's constantly on the alert.
You can't edge past
its arm of fierce blown air
and then not write a cheque
or set a payment up.

Sometimes you feel, can't I
live a fairly blameless life
and that's enough?
But the drier won't have it:
it spots you washing
your hands of gift-aid, care, concern
and booms the shame of it
to everyone, to bring-and-buyers,
lickers of little envelopes,
the relentless good.

UNSEENS

Each week we'd bring an unseen home,
a passage for translation.
It might be prose or verse.
Meanings, our tutor told us,
would lead to meanings
which would lead to meanings.
Left in the sudden dark
we stared as though our stare
would spring a leak of light
beneath a door or curtain
and we'd understand. Feeling
ahead of us, still blind,
we must have blundered
through emptinesses
where the dark was darkest.
Somewhere there'd be meanings
which would lead to meanings.

WASH

After a boat goes past
its wash sets off

across the calm grey silk
toward you. Frothy

to be told, story
after story arches in.

To be a coast or shore
must be to let each wave

ungulp its passionate say
and then slip backward

from you down your rocks
translucent, listened to.

from OWL SONGS (2021)

OWL

The poem that our local
tawny owl half-croons,
half-whistles in the dark,
is, like almost every
other poem, the echo
of an earlier noise
like clattering through branches,
the breathy send-and-take
of mating-calls or the sound
that silence makes when,
sculpted in oak, an owl
waits by its tree-hole
for the light to fade.

HANDS

> 'In addition to their property as tools hands have something like their own soul.' Karl Schleffler

You don't see souls when hands
are gripping on to, digging
over, working at. Best
when they're lying empty
on a table, not stretched flat
but with the knuckles raised enough
to hide a thing that isn't
there. The fingers draw a bony
curtain down to cover it
so you can't, except in woodcuts,
paintings, photographs see in.
Finding souls in things, I've never thought,
must be what art is for.

IN THE ALPUJARRAS

Trees for flowers in this garden
of gardens, orange, avocado,
quince, lemon, mango and, out-
gnarling all of these, olive.
Trunks rough with trenches
and in the starry silver-green
of leaves, a wall of mountain.
The daubs of white up there
aren't snowdrifts, they're knuckles
of little painted villages
which have seen how olives
hook themselves to rocky
hillsides and cling on and on.

ON A LEVEL-CROSSING

Please don't think that stretch
of startled life you wrote about
has rattled past and gone.
One stretch of life can work
another loose with wanting
to be lived again. I know
you've crossed and re-crossed
deserts, frontiers, chasms, dodgy
gaps, yet please don't miss
what level-crossings like the one
you're inching over currently
say in France: 'A train can hide
the fact another train is coming.'

WAVES BREAKING

Open all night
the double doors of our balcony
overhearing the sea.
Soon there'll be nothing left
in our heads but waves,
the breaking and pounding
of waves. Easy to hear
without listening; easy to miss,
in all that same old thunder,
the little scuttle of stones
which must have thought
this time they'd get away,
they were half-way up the beach.

NIBBLING

Someone prone to loyalty and mischief
took a day off work
to be there for his friend and flatmate
at the immigration court.
Warm in the pocket of his coat
he held a fieldmouse
which during the proceedings
nibbled oats. Like but unlike
the nibbling at the now 800-
year-old process of the law,
the right of everyone
to justice without (the word
is almost nibbled through) delay.

BEING HEARD

You listen and you make me think
my story's everything,
you need each word I say.
What I need is to be listened to
so openly your listening
swallows words my throat
still can't not choke at; what
I need is for the nothing
in my head that waits
to horrify me till I fall
asleep, to sleep itself,
be nothing but a word
with spelling and no spell.

RAIN
for Alison, Hilary, Andrew, Elinor

A thunderstorm and then
a simple storm. This is how
rain should come, straight down
without bluster or sudden
angled squalls. It might be
falling upward it's so mild.
Sons and daughters know by its
existence or its non-existence
there's a love like this: straight
down, an equal easy rain.
They also know a father's ignorance
of what he's really like
rains just as steadily.

MUD
for my sister, Mary

You don't much like perfection.
Mud's perfect though when,
on an almost lightless day,
the low tide's left a glassy rink
with waders on it that don't wade
but step across its surface
spearing things. It's changeable,
this mud, you have to catch it
moist and white and preferably
with avocets sliding their up-
turned beaks about in it. Your
painting's wonderful: quiet,
totally modest, almost perfect.

REFLEX

Words, you used to say,
are waiting, all you do
is choose. Until one day
you didn't choose but tapped
and saw your foot fly up
without you helping it
as if it wasn't yours.
You know you can't allow
a thought to intervene
excusing or retracting,
you haven't time to lie.
Your foot's too quick for you,
too truthful, too obedient.

from COUNTRY OF ARRIVAL
(2022)

TO SWIM

Sometimes you can't let go
of the ladder and when you do

you splash off backward
for a stroke or two then

struggle back. You don't
go anywhere that's not

provisional, anywhere
you can't get back from

to a blank white page.
To set off across the lake

and let the breathing
of your whispered words

transport you, take you stroke
by stroke, each line of you

easing through nothingness
and into each next line,

that would be buoyancy,
that would be to swim.

CROSSING BLIND

The stranded ones not even
written yet and not
yet smuggled through

are crossing blind.
They have a still sea-mist
to blind them, to let them

work their way across
unseen. It's no good
if they set their sights

on endings, on white cliffs.
They've no sights to set,
they've nothing but a sea

of little chasms behind them
opened like mouths, like wounds
closed over now,

and underneath their boat
a sea of stillness
to be paddled through.

CONSULTATION DOCUMENT

Gangs of rodents
are ripping down our fences,
burrowing under, letting
lambs come in. We've always
loved our lambs but this time
for safety's sake and to ensure
the gangs of criminals
leave our shores for ever
the government has decided
to eliminate all lambs.
Full compensation will be paid
to butchers, owners of abattoirs,
sheep-farmers. The government
values your opinion. Please
tick the appropriate box.
How effective do you think
the decision to eliminate
lambs will be (a) effective
(b) very effective (c) very very effective?

SNAKES AND LADDERS

You thought you'd learned to play
the games dictators play.

Hide and Seek of course though
Hide and Not Be Found is where

you kept your special skill.
One morning you weren't anywhere.

When the men came seeking
you'd already carried off

your freedom in a little
boat. U.K. you came to but

you'd hardly got here when quite
courteously they asked you to play

Snakes and Ladders with them. It
was Snakes for you. You travelled

in a boat so dangerous, they said,
you have to leave at once.

You should have come by ladder,
arriving at Heathrow.

IN THE MIST

Out in the mist toward Essex
fifty or so on a windfarm.

Long lean blades revolving
over the grey of the sea. No

leaking dinghies, no border-
boats swooping to stop them.

The earthly, the un-
miraculous, flounders here,

can't share the same sea
as these mildly proceeding

walkers on water. Dear
refugees in the mist, walk

on water across to us,
save us, save us from us.

ALL THE DIFFERENCE

A man we know
knows all the difference
difference can make. Iraqi Kurd
trained as a paramedic in Iraq,
refugee to Britain, carer,
Care Home Manager now.

Fifteen years ago was taken
handcuffed from a cell in Colnbrook
to be deported. A friend, a lawyer
and a technicality slipped in
across the border and with only
minutes till the plane took off

saved him. He knew all
the difference then and knew
it too when on the 1st of March
this year, not on the 23rd,
he chose with full approval
from the relatives his Care Home's

own lockdown. The difference
that the difference made is like
taut-stretched razor-wire
between this and that. Carers
and cared for, not one became
infected, not one died.

THE TOPPLING

Never thought we'd live to see
it actually topple over.
Upturned the statue fell
across the square, its uprightness
in pieces, skidding, strewn
amongst us. On a slab worked
loose, 'In recognition,' it says,
'of the achievement' (maybe
they'll lock the plaque away
until we need to say such things
again) 'of establishing
in the heart of Africa
detention camps for illegal
immigrants to Britain.'

LEAVE TO REMAIN

Leave to remain is everything
and nothing. It's what you long for
but its small print doesn't
mention what you leave behind
when you remain.

Home smells, the lingering
of sounds. Some have to tell
themselves they'll never pass
their new-born child across
to grandparents to hold.

Every refugee has the story
of a refugee behind them.
How to leave your story,
leave the name of refugee
behind and be, happen

to be a person who drives taxis,
a person watching swans
fly overhead, a person
whose first thought on waking
is of a sleeping child.

GIFTS FROM AUSTRALIA

You loved Australia,
you brought back brightly painted
boomerangs in plenty
for your English friends.

I still don't understand
why when you throw them
boomerangs skim off and round
and back to you, why

when you're back in London
and we hear you're using
your Uber-driving earnings
to rebuild damaged

wells in villages in Darfur
we can't help welling too
with, is it pride, this
brightly painted gift

you left us with or
is it your great-heartedness,
lonely, skimming back
to find us now you're gone?

SCARS OF NOT
for Sharif Barko (1962–2021)

We weren't there
when they shot you dead
three thousand miles away.
Safe in our beds at home
we still weren't out of range.

The last live picture
has you sitting totally
unsafe at ease among
your friends. Your smile straight
at the camera lures us

across to feel your hug
of reassurance round us.
We come to your memorial
sitting at a screen
where no one sees

the scars, the bullet-wounds
of loving you, of having
no burn-marks on our backs,
of not being tortured,
not shot dead ourselves.

THE HEART AND THE HEARING
for Danyah

The doctors at the hospital
closed the hole in your heart
and opened up your hearing.

Now you can start again.
When you get home there'll be
soft nonsense – can you hear it? –

coming from your parents.
There'll be the little trills
of sound your brothers make.

They're words, the sort of music
you'll be playing soon. Don't
think of meanings. The heart

will understand. Your ears
throbbing with endearments,
your heart hearing.

UNMUTED

When we got to school
they ticked our names off,
muted us although
we hardly needed it,
the other frightened boys
and I in 1945, set us
a hymn to sing, some
education to be going
on with and we floated
silently along with it
where we were pointed.

Unmuting someone
can't be done to order,
switching on or off. All
we did was face the other
way. We hardly made
a splash for twenty
years and then in rougher
narrower water
a jam of logs came
bursting down my river
jostling to be said.

LAW

Our Latin teacher only
had initials, didn't have
a first name or a surname,
only LAW. He'd written
books on Latin grammar
which we learnt for homework.
Learn by heart, he'd tell us,
all the Latin prepositions
and which case they take.
He was our preposition.
We came after him, his
Cases, his Accusatives,
his Ablatives. Never
suspected there'd be
other laws of grammar
waiting to be followed
if ever what we needed
was to write our minds.

COLD BATHS
at a Methodist boys' boarding school 1950

At 6 a.m. John Wesley used to tip-
toe through our dormitory
and run our baths for us.

Cold baths, I can hear the steady
deepening of the water's voice
as the baths filled.

We didn't mind the cold,
kept our gasps to ourselves.
Quite soon we'd toughen up

and not know what gasps were.
We didn't have to feel
our feelings, we needn't

tremble, blush or weep.
We could keep a safe white
silence going for weeks.

THE ONLY PLACE

The only place of safety
is the poem itself. You flee
from speechlessness, white spaces,
and if you're lucky the city
of sanctuary takes you in.

If you're lucky there's no leak
in the boat you've hired,
no avalanche blocking the path
you take across the mountains,
no border guard awake

and no righteous booted men
climbing your precipice of stairs
at 5 a.m., kicking your door in,
twisting your words until
they howl their innocence.

Once inside your room, inside
your table-lamp's kind glow,
you learn to mean the words
your poem speaks for you, your
lines go sauntering out

across the chasms of white
silence that you fled from.
Asylum is an ink
you dip your pen into
and write your leave to remain.

FIELD OF VISION

The field of vision
that gloved and padded up
you walk out on to
at the ophthalmologist's
operates through sparks of light
appearing and you acknowledging
every spark you see.

Gully, mid-off, mid-on
you can't help seeing them.
It's deep square leg, deep extra cover, deep third man
that interest the ophthalmologist.

Maybe I did miss them. Maybe my field
of vision's getting narrower
and in the end the only
spark I'll see is
silly point.

AS GOLDFINCHES

As goldfinches take care
to pause in nearby bushes
before darting out
to peck at sunflower hearts
and spit away the husks

so trains from Paddington
are careful or they used to be
to pause beside a cemetery
until the signal nods
and lets them into Oxford.

Always check on the dead
is good advice. Make sure
your parents are as you left them
in your nearby mind,
lovingly remembered and

forgotten. Hearts and husks.

WORK IN PROGRESS

Looks like grief in progress,
the wheelbarrow abandoned
half-way down the garden,
half-way across. Was it
on its way to being tipped
up, left leaning forward
on a shed with paint-pots,
an old cupboard, broken chairs
inside? Was grief suddenly
too much to push around?
What sometimes works with grief
and wheelbarrows is turning round
and pulling, taking the weight
behind you till you're almost
happy knowing by heart.

from HELLO DEAR (2023)

HELLO DEAR

> *The title refers to the greeting in a message written by a girl detained, amongst other refugees, at Manston Processing Centre in Kent in autumn 2022. She threw her letter, pleading for help, over the fence in a bottle. Learn more here:*

Hello dear. The message
in the bottle, addressed to
*Journalists, Organisations,
Everyone*, spoke to us
kindly as though we were
a child, a single child.

The single child who'd done
the job of throwing
the message in the bottle
over the wire to where
*Journalists, Organisations,
Everyone* stood waiting

was one of *Everyone*.
Hello dear we adult everyones
might murmur through the fence
to her. She said it first though,
seemed to know it first
that everyone was dear.

LONG SLOW FALL

Seems like this afternoon
not twenty years ago I
last fell off my bike.
It happened slowly, slowly
came to me my front wheel
was going somewhere else,
was jammed in one direction
while I went in the other.
Was gravity off duty
letting me think my thoughts
before I fell? It didn't flash,
my plan for a safe landing,
it lumbered through my head.
Would broken ribs be preferable
to a broken wrist? Once
you let your handlebars
go loose, might you save your arms,
crash-landing on your chest?
All this you're given time for
between what happens and
what's bound to happen after it.

DOUBLE-ENDED SAW

in memory of Peter Rowe

Your father-in-law, you said,
vicarious father, vicar,
used a double-ended saw
for log-cutting when you stayed.
On ordinary days he kept
his sawing and next Sunday's
sermon to himself. But when
you came, he had a feast
in store, a to-and-fro
of thought proposed, responded to,
about religion, a to-and-fro
of pauses while the saw
continued cutting in its sleep
and you two worked at thinking.

Later most of us hung up
our saws except we went
on sawing, not slicing through
but going slightly deeper.

DAWDLING
in memory of my late wife, Diana

You burst out once and said
I went too fast. Couldn't I
forget where we were going
and go slower, look at things?
Couldn't I dawdle sometimes
like you did? That was more
than twenty years ago since
when you've sped away from me
and I from you. I don't
think either of us thought
we'd go so far so quickly
from each other. Now that
the only being left to you
is being remembered, I want
to tell you I'm clinging to you,
going slowly, dawdling
as you race away through time.

WHY WOULD THE ROAD?

Why would the road from the village
slope down so steeply
if it didn't want you to follow,
free-wheeling if you have wheels?

And why would it then lead you
through a tunnel of green
so thick-knit you feel
your way through the night of it

if you didn't come through the trees
into the dazzle of ordinary,
clouds as clouds are I suppose
when no one's looking at them?

BALANCING ACT

It must be true, it's there
in black and white, a photograph
of Nolde's fifty years younger
second wife holding a cup
of tea up on her finger-
tips. Nolde and she are sitting
in his studio, paintings
like naughty children lined up
in front of them. Nolde
loved Germany, had high hopes
of Hitler. Hitler called
his art degenerate though,
even stopped him painting.
He looks inscrutably across
at her. Along the wall,
standing shoulder-to-shoulder
almost joined, sea-spray,
huge rumbling skies, flowers.

WEATHER AND NEWS

'Weather and news, Gertie,'
my grandfather called to his sister
on September 3rd just before
9 p.m.. Every evening
he would do the same
and we'd sit round in the last
of the light, in the almost
silent film of ourselves
on September 3rd, hearing
the news. I can't recall
a word the wireless said.
Someone must have told me
we were going to be fighting
a war and my great-aunt
went gently round lighting
the gas on the walls. I
think there were little hisses
at first then each hiss
burst out into a flame.

LIME-GRIEF
for Bridget Rowe

Lime-trees can't be faulted
in the way they grieve.

Deciduous and lofty
perhaps they find it easy

to forget the past, which
anyway took place modestly

a hundred feet below.
Lime-trees remind us though:

the honeydew that insects
suck from them in summer

oozes out and sticks
to surfaces it falls on,

on car-bonnets and on the thin
skin of our sense that we

were with you once, at ease,
at what seemed our best.

BUTCHER'S NAME

I forget the name of the butcher
in the Oxford Covered Market
where we bought our weekend meat.
I remember the meat.
I remember how, playing
the organ at our church
on Sunday mornings, there
he was, our butcher, not
a trace of blood, I see,
smearing the keys. Even now
meat, Oxford, religion
spill out on each other as I carve them
clear of my life. No more
non-conformist hymns, no more punt-
poles stuck in Cherwell mud,
no more Lindsay's sausages.
There, I've remembered the name.

COLLISIONS

I still keep voices of small boats
especially of punts and rowing-boats
softly colliding with each other
in my head. These days collisions
happen much more angrily. It seems
our Threatforce wants a not
too public way of pushing boats
they don't approve of back
across the sea. I hope they don't
use poles like those we used to stir
up mud-clouds as we pushed
our lovers up and down the river
in a punt. These orange-jacketed
arrivers bring their own home
voices with them in their heads,
their soft collisions. A sloping beach
growls at them as they land.

HUMANITY

Seems the word humanity
has been deleted, can't be
used in argument any more.
Money we can handle,
count it up and say
how much it is. Human-
ity is not like that, it can't
mount up on money-changers'
tables, it doesn't when
the tables are upturned
go skidding off across the temple
floor. Humanity can still
be handcuffed though, blind-
folded, flown off to Rwanda.

NO TALKING BEFORE BREAKFAST

Love, I'm sorry but I like
our wordlessness when dozing
to go on unbroken until
almost breakfast-time. No
stories before 8 a.m., no quotes
from books you've woken to,
no dreams recounted. It's
words I'm thinking of.
Maybe we hear so harshly
in harsh morning light
words shrivel, lose their shape.
After 8 is fine. By then a word
has woken, is renewed, silvered
in the salt of dozing, stay-
ing under, swimming through
the swirl, the blur of it.
By then a word can speak.

MOON POEM

You'll be at the bedroom window now
marvelling. You've always loved
the moon. Back here in hospital

a pillow I keep on a ledge
at the top of the bed, next
to my head, drops lightly onto me.

Being in hospital's a marvel
when you rest your hand
on my shoulder like that.

NO FEAR

I remember thinking, now
there's nothing to fear.
That was twenty years ago,
it's out of date. The man
in the bed next to me
shouts at night for his sons.
I haven't said it but I've
told him all he can do
is murmur the names or think them.
Out of date is when you drift
into a different reach
of being, of no date at all,
no remembering, no shouting
through a night impenetrable
as this. Nothing left to fear.